SWANSEA'S ANTARCTIC EXPLORER

Frontispiece. Edgar Evans as a gunnery rating. This picture used to hang in the hall of his old school, St Helen's, in Vincent Street. (SM)

SWANSEA'S ANTARCTIC EXPLORER
Edgar Evans, 1876–1912

G.C. Gregor

CITY OF SWANSEA

1995

To: Rachel, Matthew, Hannah, Elizabeth, Jonathan

The publication of this book by Swansea City Council does not necessarily imply the Council's official approbation of the opinions expressed herein.

First published 1995 by Swansea City Council.
Obtainable from the City Archives Office, Central Services Department, Guildhall, Swansea, SA1 4PE.

City Archives Publications: Studies in Swansea's History, no. 4.

ISBN 0 946001 28 6

General Editor:
J.R. Alban, B.A., Ph.D., D.A.A., *City Archivist.*

Contents

		Page
List of Illustrations		vii
Abbreviations		ix
General Editor's Preface		xi
Foreword and Acknowledgements		xiii
Introduction		xv
Chapter 1:	The Early Years	1
Chapter 2:	The *Discovery*	13
Chapter 3:	Marriage	23
Chapter 4:	The *Terra Nova*	29
Chapter 5:	Antarctica, 1911	40
Chapter 6:	The Southern Journey	52
Chapter 7:	The Relief Expedition	64
Chapter 8:	Lois	70
Chapter 9:	Recognition	78
Chapter 10:	The Best Choice?	88
Appendix 1:	Chronology	91
Appendix 2:	Sledge Parties	93
Appendix 3:	'The Martyred Hero of Antarctica'	95
Appendix 4:	Locations of Memorabilia	100
Select Bibliography		101

List of Illustrations

		Page
Frontispiece.	Edgar Evans as a gunnery rating	ii
Figure 1.	Map of south-west Gower	2
Figure 2.	Charles Evans, father of Edgar, in 1893	4
Figure 3.	Edgar Evans and his elder sister, Annie, in 1893	6
Figure 4.	The Head Post Office, Castle Bailey Street, Swansea in the 1880s	8
Figure 5.	The Castle Hotel, Swansea, 1895	9
Figure 6.	Map of Swansea in 1883	10
Figure 7.	RRS *Discovery* in May 1928	16
Figure 8.	Edgar Evans's discharge certificate, 1904	21
Figure 9.	Edgar Evans in 1904	24
Figure 10.	St Mary's church, Rhosili	26
Figure 11.	Royal naval gun crew, 1907	27
Figure 12.	Menu from the farewell banquet at the Royal Hotel, Cardiff, 13 June 1910	32
Figure 13.	The first page of Edgar Evans's last letter to his mother	42
Figure 14.	The *Terra Nova* in Antarctica	48
Figure 15.	The western and depot parties	53
Figure 16.	Edgar Evans bandaging Surgeon-Lieut. Atkinson's frostbitten hand, 5 July 1911	54
Figure 17.	Map of the route to the Pole	56
Figure 18.	Herbert Ponting's 1911 photograph of PO Edgar Evans	58
Figure 19.	At the South Pole, 18 January 1912	62
Figure 20.	Plaque inside Rhosili church	75
Figure 21.	'Antarctic heroes' postcard	79

Figure 22.   Philip Chatfield's bust of Edgar Evans   80
Figure 23.   Plaque in the foyer of the Edgar Evans Building,
              Whale Island, Portsmouth   90

Abbreviations

CDL   *Cambria Daily Leader*
SPRI   Scott Polar Research Institute, University of Cambridge
SM   Swansea Museum
SWDP   *South Wales Daily Post*
SWEP   *South Wales Evening Post*
WM   *Western Mail*

General Editor's Preface

Captain Scott's Antarctic expedition of 1910–13 has a well recorded place in the annals of international history and polar exploration. The heroism of the polar party and their self-sacrifice have long been regarded as inspirational examples of the British character and spirit. Small wonder that the expedition has been the subject of numerous studies in the course of the twentieth century, although those which have appeared in later years have tended to reassess the story to a degree. What is perhaps not so widely known is that one of that ill-fated polar party was a Swansea man, Chief Petty Officer Edgar Evans. Nevertheless, while Evans's name is not so universally famous as those of Scott, Oates, Bowers, and Wilson, it is familiar to many in Swansea and in his native Gower. However, even in Swansea, his *actual* exploits are not so well known. While many are aware of his presence in the ill-fated expedition of 1910–13, few realise that he had, for example, accompanied Scott on an earlier Antarctic expedition in 1901–4 or that he was an effective naval gunnery instructor, his gun crews winning the prize for field gunnery at the Royal Naval Tattoos of 1906 and 1907. Indeed, it is an unfortunate fact that official recognition of him locally was exceedingly slow in coming.

In view of the central part which he played in such an important episode of exploration and in view of the fact that that role has been largely overlooked by other writers who tended to concentrate on the officers in the party, it is clear that a comprehensive biography of Edgar Evans is long overdue. Since Evans is one of a small group of famous Swansea people, the 'Studies in Swansea's History' series has been seen as a fitting place for such a biography to appear. The author, Gary Gregor, himself a Swansea native, and a member of the Captain Scott Society, has, for many years, been interested in Evans and has researched and written extensively on the man. He is therefore well placed to produce this biography.

Previous volumes in the 'Studies in Swansea's History' series have tended to deal mainly with aspects of the social history of the city, so, in many respects, the inclusion of a biography in the series is a new departure. Readers will find that most of the 'action' of the present work takes place away from Swansea. However, such a study is nonetheless relevant, since it documents the activities of a famous son of Swansea on the stage of international events. It also deals with Edgar Evans's early life in Gower and Swansea and shows his continuing links and those of his wife, Lois, with this part of south Wales. It is hoped that this work will deservedly bring Edgar Evans's exploits to the attention of a wider audience.

J.R. Alban

Foreword and Acknowledgements

In the course of writing this book I can identify with the feeling of John Petts, sculptor and stained glass artist, who said that the implication of many of the works which he was called upon to make reduced him to a midget.[1] The story of that epic trek to 90 degrees South (which figures large in the following pages) is about far more than physical effort, and to dismiss it with such a phrase as, 'There's no success like failure...'[2] is the superficial comment of a cynic. Not having myself ventured further south than the Cape of Good Hope, nor having served in the Royal Navy, my recent efforts (such as swimming 5km or running a half marathon) to identify with some of the physical demands of that trek were hopelessly inadequate. But while accompanying an aid convoy from Swansea to Bosnia came the realisation that the distance which we travelled comparatively easily was the same as that which Edgar Evans and his four companions had covered — over eighty years ago, in Antarctica, and on foot! It was then that something of the magnitude of their undertaking reached me. So my acknowledgements must start with those men, three of whom had been on a lengthy sledging trip during the earlier expedition (and still they went back again).

While not presuming to claim any literary merit in this book, I am nonetheless pleased that it is published during the year in which Swansea hosts the UK Year of Literature.

To refer throughout to the subject of this book as Edgar, rather than by his surname, may seem excessively informal, but it does avoid confusion with Lieutenant 'Teddy' Evans in the later part.

I would particularly like to thank Dr John Alban, City Archivist, for his constructive observations and publishing expertise, Dr Geoffrey Hattersley-

Smith, Mrs Ellen-Johanne McGhie, and HMSO for permission to include extracts from the English translation of Major Gran's diary, the Curator and staff of Swansea Museum for access to relevant material, Mrs Viv Lewis for the maps and Mr Paul Jenkins for the cover illustration. As an acknowledgement of his preliminary work thirty years ago, the appendix includes Mr Stanley Richards's article, first published in the *South Wales Evening Post*. Finally, thanks to my wife Jane for her constant support and encouragement throughout.

NOTES

1. *Artists in Wales*, ed. M. Stephens (Llandysul, 1977). The 1965 'Wales for Alabama' window is the supreme example of what John Petts meant.

2. Bob Dylan in 'Love Minus Zero/No Limit', from *Bringing it All Back Home* (CBS, 1965).

Introduction

Two peacetime tragedies which occurred within weeks of each other in 1912 are rarely out of the news for long, even towards the close of the twentieth century.

The impact of the sinking of SS *Titanic* in the north Atlantic on the night of 14/15 April during her maiden voyage exceeded even the loss of 1,513 lives, for there have been larger maritime disasters. It represented a watershed in British society, signalling the dismantling of Edwardian self-confidence and complacency. The boast that 'Not even God could sink this ship' did not require any Divine response: human ambition, together with disregard for iceberg warnings, sufficed.

When, ten months later, the news came through of an earlier tragedy on the other side of the globe—the death of by contrast a mere five men during an Antarctic expedition—the impact was no less. Four days later ten thousand people stood outside St Paul's Cathedral during a memorial service attended by King George V for Captain Robert Falcon Scott and his four companions. The story of their sufferings and comradeship, as revealed in the journals found beside Scott's body, was an inspiration particularly to those called upon to serve their country in both World Wars, as well as to countless other persons. Even this more cynical present age, which calls into question Scott's motives and leadership abilities (issues which are vigorously defended, incidentally[1]), has not diminished fascination in the epic 1910–13 expedition and its ramifications.

The three men who died together—Scott, Wilson and Bowers—have rightly received much attention in memorials and literature, as has the person whose earlier death became a byword for self-sacrifice and heroism—Captain Oates. But the fifth member of that party, who had stood together at the South Pole in January 1912, has been comparatively ignored—relegated to the role of, at best, a minor participant, at worst, the weak link whose collapse and death jeopardised the lives of his four comrades.

Such views render a grave disservice to the sole Welshman among the Polar party. This book is no exercise in hero-worship: rather it is the account of a man with human faults and failings, but possessing a strong heart and body, a person of immense loyalty and character, who was an integral member of the 1910 British Antarctic Expedition—Chief Petty Officer Edgar Evans.

NOTE

1. For example, see articles by Wayland Young (Lord Kennet) in *Encounter* (May 1980 and November 1980).

CHAPTER 1

The Early Years

During much of the nineteenth century, the port of Swansea in south Wales was the world centre for the smelting of copper. Since approximately two tons of coal were needed to smelt one ton of copper ore, it was economical to site a copper works near an abundant coal supply. The Lower Swansea Valley provided this, and a copper works had been sited there from as early as 1717. With coal seams running down to the banks of the River Tawe, vessels could sail across the Bristol Channel to obtain ore from the Cornish mines. When these became worked out, vessels sailed further afield — to Anglesey, to Cuba, and eventually to the countries on the west coast of South America, principally Chile.

So throughout that century copper barques laden with coal would sail from Swansea across the Atlantic Ocean and round Cape Horn, in order to obtain copper ore. Those hardy seamen were known as the Swansea 'Cape Horners'.[1] Their voyages — of at least six months' duration — were hazardous undertakings. Those who managed to safely round Cape Horn then faced the perils of disease in the South American ports, and even the possibility of spontaneous combustion of the coal cargo after the lengthy voyage: finally Cape Horn had to be rounded again on the return journey.

One such Cape Horner was the father of Edgar Evans, Charles Evans, who came from Oxwich in the south of Gower, the peninsula to the west of Swansea. Charles was the second son of Thomas Evans,[2] a quarryman, for, from the late eighteenth century, limestone used to be quarried from the Oxwich and Rhosili cliffs, to be shipped across the Bristol Channel for using on the fields of North Devon.[3] Three previous generations of the Evans family were all from the nearby village of Penrice, just inland from Oxwich.[4]

On 24 July 1862,[5] when he was aged twenty-three, Charles Evans married Sarah Beynon at St Mary's Church in Rhosili, the village near the

tip of south-west Gower. The parish of Rhosili at that time had sixty-four
inhabited houses, with a population of 294.[6] Charles's profession was given
as mariner, with his residence being Oxwich. His bride, Sarah, was then
aged twenty-two, the daughter of William Beynon, licensee of the 'Ship
Inn' at Middleton, the next hamlet to the east. Beynon is a well-known
Gower name, well represented among the gravestones in Rhosili
churchyard. For most of the nineteenth century the Beynon family held the
licence of the 'Ship Inn',[7] with it later passing to Sarah's brother—another
William Beynon: one of his daughters, Lois, would later marry her cousin
Edgar Evans. The wedding of Charles Evans and Sarah Beynon was
performed by Revd John Ponsonby Lucas, Rector of Rhosili and
Llangennith. His rectory was situated in splendid isolation midway between
the two parishes, overlooking Rhosili Bay.

    Charles and Sarah Evans settled in the village, where their first child was
born in 1864, and given the names of his father and maternal grandfather,
William Charles. He was baptised in the church on 3 April. There may have
followed some stillbirths or deaths in infancy, all too common in those
days, for their next surviving child was John Austin, born in 1867. By the
time Mary Anne was born the following year, the family had moved to
nearby Middleton, settling at Fernhill Top Cottage, a short walk inland
from the 'Ship Inn'. Another daughter, Annie Jane, was born in 1870, so

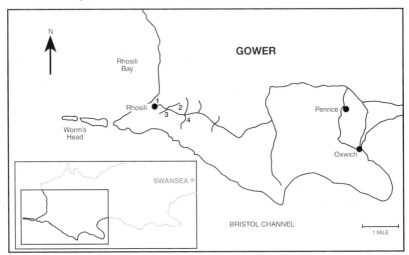

Figure 1.   Map of south-west Gower, showing: 1. Rhosili church; 2. Fernhill Top;
*   3. the 'Ship Inn'; 4. Pitton*   (Viv Lewis)

that the 1871 census records Charles aged seven, John aged four, and their sisters aged two and one. A third son Arthur was born in 1874, and then on 7 March 1876 into this family of three boys and two girls was born Edgar. At the time of her confinement with Edgar Mrs Sarah Evans was staying at nearby Middleton Cottage with her sister Elizabeth, wife of shoemaker William Morgan. [8]

Mrs Sarah Evans registered the birth on 13 April 1876, [9] and Edgar was baptised at Rhosili church at the end of that month. If born on the 7 March he would have shared his birthday with the present-day Antarctic explorer Sir Ranulph Fiennes; but his Naval record states that Edgar was born on 9 March, and he evidently adhered to this in Antarctica during the first geological journey of 1911.

Sarah Evans did not sign her name on the birth certificate, but if at that time she was illiterate, it was no disgrace, a mere six years after Forster's Education Act. At that time south-west Gower was quite remote, with the road from Swansea ending at Pitton Cross: travellers for Pitton, Middleton and Rhosili had to brave a narrow lane, high-banked and muddy, and just wide enough for a horse and cart. [10]

A younger brother, George, was born in 1878, and a third daughter, Eliza Jane, the following year. [11] By 1881, the family had moved to Pitton, the next hamlet to the east, and the census describes seven-year old Arthur and five-year old Edgar as scholars, and lists George aged three and Eliza Jane aged one. Of the four eldest children, it could be that Charles and John, then aged seventeen and fourteen, had left home, and thirteen-year old Mary Anne and eleven-year old Annie might have been elsewhere that day.

In 1883 the family moved the twelve miles east into Swansea, for by then Charles Evans was engaged in comparatively local work, with Bacon's boats (later Coast Lines Ltd), as quartermaster in the *Sunlight*, on what was known as the 'Glasgow Trade'. [12] The town's population at this time was over 50,000 and increasing; smoke and pollution from the copper works affected those who lived on the east side. But the Evans family settled initially in Hoskins Place, off lower Oxford Street, moving later to nearby William Street. [13] Even so, it must have been a sharp contrast to rural Gower.

Edgar attended St Helens School in Vincent Street from the age of six until he was thirteen. Opened in 1874 after W.E. Forster's Elementary

Figure 2.   Charles Evans, father of Edgar, in 1893.   (Keith Roberts)

Education Act of 1870, the school had nearly 250 pupils in 1883 when Edgar first went there, but as the town expanded with the industrial developments the number grew to over 350 by the time he left. The headmaster was Mr Lewis Schleswick, who was to occupy that position from 1880 for nearly forty years. [14]

For pupils punctuality often depended on the accuracy of the Swansea hospital clock, which could frequently be slow. Attendances were affected by illnesses such as typhoid fever, of which there was an outbreak in the district during the autumn of 1886, and scarlet fever, two years later.

St Helen's School is in the area known as the Sandfields, and games periods were held on the nearby sands of Swansea Bay. The town had a severe drought during the summer of 1887, and exceptionally hot summers in the late 1880s made it difficult to keep pupils working. At such times the end of the school day signalled a rush to the nearby sands.

By 1887 the boys were receiving three-quarters of an hour's instruction in military drill every Tuesday morning, from 10.00 to 10.45 am. In June of that year the pupils marched in procession to the opening of the Public Free Library in Alexandra Road. One imagines that the pupils had dispersed to enjoy a half-holiday by the time W.E. Gladstone (then out of office, but later to serve a fourth term as Prime Minister) delivered a speech on the Irish Home Rule issue.

There would have been frequent visits to the relatives in Gower, especially to the Beynons at the 'Ship Inn' in Middleton. Eleven-year old Edgar would have often gone onto Rhosili Beach to see the dwindling hulk of the Norwegian barque the *Helvetia*, which had run aground during a storm on 28 October 1887. Its cargo of wood had been unloaded on the beach, but there had been no loss of life, unlike so many of the shipwrecks around the Gower coast.

Those times saw much exploitation of children as cheap labour, although the 1874 Factory Act had raised the age at which they could be employed as 'half-timers' (spending half their time in school and half in employment) from eight to ten years old. So, possibly from as early as 1886, Edgar may have become a telegraph messenger boy at Swansea's Head Post Office, then in Castle Bailey Street, beside the ruins of Swansea Castle. That Head Post Office was to move in December 1901 to Wind Street, on the site of

Figure 3.   Edgar Evans and his elder sister, Annie, in 1893.   (Keith Roberts)

the old coaching inn, the Mackworth Hotel. In those later premises Henry Chapman's 1904 photograph of Edgar was displayed for many years.

A Gower man, George Richards, was Head Postmaster, well disposed to employing persons from that area.[15] In Edgar's time messenger boys still started each day with musket duty, for the building adjoined the Drill Hall. Something of Edgar's character can be gauged from an incident at that time. Behind the Post Office the ground sloped away to the North Dock, created in 1852 after the River Tawe had been diverted by what became known as the 'New Cut'. Vessels from exotic destinations would tie up in the North Dock, as recorded by some early photographs of Revd Calvert Richard Jones. Young lads used to gather round the boats, plying the sailors with questions, and sometimes being permitted to step on board. Perhaps it was after one such diversion that Edgar returned to the telegraph office soaking wet, having fallen in the dock.[16] However he made light of his misadventure — good character training for a person who as a mariner would experience many occasions of being wet through, with no opportunity for hours or even days to get dry or to change into dry clothing.

The mariner's lot was succinctly described by a Captain John Smith in 1627: 'Men of all other professions, in lightning, thunder, storms and tempest with rain and snow, may shelter themselves in dry houses, by good fires, and good cheer; but those are the chief times that seamen must stand to their tacklings, and attend with all diligence their greatest labour upon the decks'. He added that 'Especially in foul weather, the labour, hazard, wet and cold is so incredible I cannot express it'.[17]

Whatever his understanding of the hazards involved, Edgar had evidently been set on a sailor's life, although his mother tried to dissuade him, saying that having one mariner in the family was quite enough. His father was similarly discouraging, fearing some accident might overtake Edgar in the Navy: after twenty years in the *Sunlight*, Charles Evans had been incapacitated when a bale of merchandise fell on his leg; blood poisoning set in, necessitating amputation.[18] Mrs Sarah Evans said Edgar was 'always a very venturesome boy, but I never heard a word of complaint pass his lips, no matter what amount of hardships he had to endure'.[19]

Leaving school at the age of thirteen, Edgar worked at the Castle Hotel, on the corner of Castle Square and St Mary's Street (where the Midland Bank stands today). The Castle Hotel had developed from an early nineteenth-century tavern into an hotel with thirty-six bedrooms employing

Figure 4.   The Head Post Office, Castle Bailey Street, Swansea in the 1880s.
(Swansea City Archives Office)

twenty servants. In 1890 it was run by a Mrs Anne Thomas, with next door a gentlemen's furnished club affiliated to it. [20]

The hotel was patronised by captains of the copper ore barques, so it is likely that hearing their conversation would further have strengthened Edgar's resolve on a seafaring career. The 1874 Factory Act had raised the age for commencing full-time employment from thirteen to fourteen years, but on attempting to join up Edgar found that to join the Navy he needed to be fifteen. Undismayed, he returned to his employer with the words 'I am coming back to you for another year, and then I am going to the Navy'. [21]

By the time of 1891 census the Evans family was living in 4 Pilton Place, off William Street, with Arthur aged seventeen, Edgar fifteen, Eliza Jane eleven, and for once their father Charles Evans is listed. Perhaps George had died some time after his third birthday, as in 1913 Mrs Sarah Evans was to speak of having buried as many as nine of her twelve children, three having died from consumption. [22] This statement was made after the deaths of Annie in 1909 and Edgar in 1912, so it seems that only their three eldest children were alive by 1913.

Figure 5.   The Castle Hotel, Swansea, 1895.   (Swansea City Archives Office)

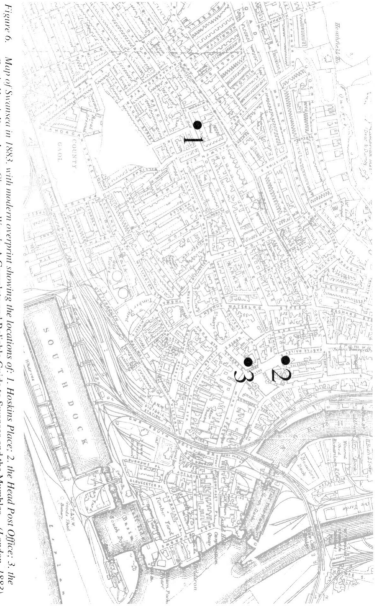

Figure 6.   Map of Swansea in 1883, with modern overprint showing the locations of: 1. Hoskins Place; 2. the Head Post Office; 3. the Castle Hotel. From James Chapman Woods, A Complete and Reliable Guide to Swansea and the Mumbles... (London, 1883), (Swansea City Archives Office)

On applying to join the Navy in 1891, Edgar's medical examination in Bristol on 5 April revealed one more decayed tooth than was permitted. Undaunted, he managed to send in a special application, which was accepted.[23] He commenced his training in HMS *Ganges*, the old hulk at Falmouth which served as the training establishment for boy cadets.[24] A year later, in April 1892, he was promoted to Boy 1st Class.

On turning eighteen in HMS *Trafalgar* in 1894 he became an Ordinary Seaman. Strongly built, he served as a physical training instructor at HMS *Excellent*, the Royal Naval Gunnery School at Whale Island, Portsmouth, and served as an Able Seaman at HMS *Vernon*.[25]

In 1898 he became a Leading Seaman when in HMS *Pembroke*, and the following year commenced two years' service in HMS *Majestic*, the flagship of the Channel Fleet. Here occurred the encounter that was to shape his destiny, for he came to the notice of a young torpedo Lieutenant, Robert Scott.

Born in Devonport, Scott had met Sir Clements Markham, President of the Royal Geographical Society, who was planning an Antarctic expedition. When Scott's offer to lead this was accepted, he decided to choose his crew from the most suitable persons he had encountered thus far in his naval career, together with those recommended by fellow officers.

NOTES

1. *Swansea Cape Horners Remember,* ed. J. Sabine and D. Hoskin (Swansea, n.d.).

2. Evans family tree, researched by Miss Eileen Evans.

3. Laurence Rich, *The Gower Peninsula* (National Trust, 1991), p. 13.

4. Evans family tree, researched by Miss Eileen Evans.

5. Copy marriage certificate, 1 November 1862.

6. Stephen Lee, 'The Population of Rhosili', *Gower*, iv (1951), 27.

7. R. Lucas, 'A Few Little Plans.... Some Sidelights on Rhosili in the 1880s and 90s, *Gower*, xliv (1993), 65.

8. *SWEP*, 11 February 1995; also letter from Cy Jones to author, 1 March 1995.

9. Copy certificate from Superintendent Registrar, 5 June 1962.

10. Rich, *The Gower Peninsula*, (National Trust, 1991), p. 17.

11. West Glamorgan County Archive Service.

12. *WM*, 12 February 1913.

13. 1891 Census; letter of Mrs S. Owen at Swansea Museum (hereafter SM); envelope 8 November 1904 at SM.

14. N.L. Thomas, *St Helen's Centenary Booklet* (Swansea, 1974).

15. Jack Bevan's recollection in J. Mansel Thomas, *Yesterday's Gower* (Llandysul, 1982), p. 155.

16. S. Richards's manuscript in SM, n.d.

17. Mason, Greenhill and Craig, *The British Seafarer* (London, 1980), Chapter 1.

18. *WM*, 12 February 1913.

19. *CDL*, 13 February 1913.

20. D.G. Bowen and N.L. Thomas, *Swansea Old and New* (Swansea, 1974).

21. *CDL*, 13 February 1913; *SWDP*, 14 February 1913.

22. *SWDP*, 18 February 1913.

23. *CDL*, 13 February 1913.

24. *Oxford Companion to Ships and the Sea* (London, 1976).

25. SM: Copy of certificate of service, June 1962.

CHAPTER 2

The *Discovery*

At the start of the twentieth century Antarctica was unknown territory. Royal Naval vessels had sailed along part of its coast, but had not penetrated the ice pack. Only an expedition led by Norwegian Carsten Borchgrevink in the *Southern Cross* in 1897–8 had set foot on the continent, and had wintered in a hut erected at Cape Adare.

The proposed National Antarctic Expedition under Commander Scott, which took place between 1901 and 1904, was to be exploratory and scientific. It was composed predominantly of Royal Naval men (thirty-eight out of forty-seven), with five scientists—a botanist, geologist, physicist, zoologist and a marine biologist. The physicist was twenty-five year old Louis Bernacchi, who had been a member of the *Southern Cross* Expedition, and who was to take charge of magnetic observations. The zoologist and assistant surgeon was Edward Wilson, aged twenty-eight, who was later to perish alongside Scott in 1912.

The six officers included a merchant naval Sub-Lieutenant who would himself become an outstanding leader of Antarctic expeditions, the twenty-six year old Irishman, Ernest Shackleton.

Edgar signed on in London on 27 July 1901. Scott described him as being nearly six foot tall, weighing 12 stone 10 lbs, 'in a hard condition'. Then aged twenty-five, Edgar was one of two second class petty officers, there being three others of first class rank. Among the seamen was Frank Wild, later to accompany Shackleton in the epic crossing from Elephant Island to South Georgia, and thirty-three year old Chief Stoker William Lashly, from Hampshire. [1]

At that time the average weekly wage for a semi-skilled man was around £1 10s. 6d. An Able Seaman received 11s. 5d. a week, but, of course, incurred no expense for board and keep. As a Petty Officer Edgar received 17s. 1d., while Wilson received £4 a week, Shackleton and Bernacchi £5 each, and Commander Scott £10.

Two learned societies, the Royal Society and the Royal Geographical Society, commissioned the building of a ship which would be suitable for scientific work and Antarctic exploration. As wood gives under pressure of ice, while steel buckles, the *Discovery* was built of wood on the Tay at Dundee. 170 foot long, 736 tons, and with a massively strengthened keel, she was barque-rigged, that is, having square sails on the fore and main masts, with fore and aft sails on the mizzen mast.

In June 1901 she was towed from Dundee to London, and berthed in the East India Dock. There she was loaded with stores, and equipped for an absence of up to three years. Meanwhile dental surgeons from Guy's hospital examined the teeth of all officers and seamen, carrying out numerous fillings and extractions.

The ship's compass was swung at Spithead, and the vessel steamed into Cowes on 5 August at the time of the regatta. The day before sailing there was a visit from the then uncrowned King Edward VII, with Queen Alexandra.

However, the *Discovery* proved to be sluggish, so instead of setting a direct course from port to port she had to meander, in order to take advantage of favourable winds and currents. Following a stop at Funchal, Madeira, the vessel reached South Africa after eight weeks at sea, and put in at Simonstown, the naval base on the peninsula south of Cape Town. The ship was open to visitors, who packed in on 7 October, a Bank Holiday in the Cape. The Anglo-Boer War was continuing, and Edgar saw a camp for Boer prisoners at Simonstown. Back in England, a certain Lieutenant Oates was preparing to re-join his regiment, having been invalided home after an heroic action in the eastern Cape in March: that injury was to have fatal consequences on a later Antarctic expedition.

From South Africa the *Discovery* sailed across to New Zealand, and put in near Christchurch at Port Lyttleton, their base in the southern hemisphere. During a month's stay the vessel was unloaded, and efforts made to locate what was dubbed 'The Dundee leak', which had caused much work on the pumps during the voyage: but the efforts met with scant success. Officers and crew enjoyed lavish New Zealand hospitality during their stay, and farmers augmented the supplies with forty-five sheep, which crowded the decks.

The departure of the *Discovery* on 21 December 1901 was a festive occasion, but marred by a fatality as they left Lyttleton harbour. Encouraged by the cheering, a young seaman named Charles Bonner had climbed to the top of the mainmast, but a sudden lurch of the vessel caused him to lose his footing and he plunged to his death on the deck beneath. That tragedy provided the opportunity for an Able Seaman from HMS *Ringamoora* of the New Zealand squadron to be transferred to the *Discovery* in Bonner's place. Thomas Crean was from County Kerry, the same age as Edgar, and the two seamen became good friends. Crean would later distinguish himself along with Lashly in 1912, and also when accompanying Shackleton in the *Endeavour*.

With the vessel so heavily laden they were fortunate not to encounter heavy seas in the Southern Ocean, and were able to economise on coal by using sail often. There were some days of thick fog, when it was necessary to keep a sharp look-out for icebergs, and at such times they missed the company of the seabirds. Crossing the Antarctic Circle on 3 January 1902 they entered the pack ice, seeing seals, penguins, and the occasional sea leopard.

The availability of fresh meat caused the decks to resemble an abbatoir, with penguins and seals being killed and skinned, and some of the New Zealand sheep being converted into mutton. But it was decided to keep the latter as a luxury for the winter months, when a change of diet would be welcome. Fresh water was secured by melting snow that had fallen on top of the ice. The consumption of coal during the laboured journey through the pack ice was considerable, but fortunately they managed to get through to open sea in just five days.

An initial landing was made at Cape Adare, near a nesting ground for thousands of Adelie penguins. On the beach stood the hut used by the *Southern Cross* expedition, and overlooking the site a cross marked the grave of one member of that party — the first man to be buried in Antarctica. Before they departed a red-painted cylinder was left conspicuously in the hut, containing details of their progress thus far, as a guide for a relief ship.

Figure 7.   RRS Discovery *in May 1928.*   (Dundee Heritage Trust)

After weighing anchor on 10 January, they sailed on south, along the coast of Victoria Land to McMurdo Sound, where they encountered the Great Ice Barrier. The *Discovery* sailed along the edge of this, and a landing was made to make some ascents in a balloon. Scott went up first, and then Shackleton, who took some photographs, but the experiment was judged to be a hazardous proceeding. On 8 February they dropped anchor in McMurdo Sound, and assembled the pre-fabricated hut, along with some sheds for the scientific instruments.

The continent's dangers were soon revealed. Edgar was among a group of men who journeyed to Cape Crozier in order to place another canister in a prominent position for directing a relief ship to their location. Returning on the 11 March they were overtaken by a blizzard while descending an icy slope. Wearing loose leather ski boots, Edgar along with Lieutenant Barne and Leading Stoker Quartley slid helplessly down, until checked by soft snow on what turned out to be the edge of a cliff. The three had an anxious time clambering up a rocky ridge to find shelter under a boulder on Castle Rock. Some hours later they were roused by the ship's siren, for once the alarm had been given steam was raised in the ship to sound this. The three men made for the direction of the sound, and encountered the search party, who guided them to safety. But another member of their original group had not been so fortunate. Able Seaman George Vince had been wearing fur boots, and he had shot past the soft snow over the edge of the cliff, falling 200 feet into the icy waters below. Scott described it as 'one of our blackest days in the Antarctic'.

The behaviour of the Siberian sledge dogs puzzled the men. Any dogs that were petted or received favour were liable to be set upon by the pack. Two docile animals which had returned from a sledging trip were killed by the pack, so that it was necessary to keep the dogs chained up.

By the end of March 1902 the Antarctic winter seemed to be advancing, and they waited for the ship to become frozen in by the surrounding ice: once that had happened they could commence the routine scientific work and communicate regularly with the magnetic huts.

There was an alarm when two men set out from the hut to return to the ship. Although only facing a distance of two hundred yards, they were caught in a blizzard and became disorientated. When a search party found them they were badly frostbitten, and it became evident that even short journeys in that climate were potentially dangerous.

Daylight hours became shorter until the sun finally disappeared on 23 April, leaving them in darkness for seventeen hours each day throughout the winter. But a well-ordered routine enabled everyone to cope with the strain of those sunless months. Naval traditions and the regularity of the meals contributed to dissipating tensions during the winter confinement on board.

Each morning a party of ten would rise early to quarry blocks of ice to be melted for the water needed for drinking, cooking and washing. Hammocks were lashed up and stowed away by breakfast at 8.30 am, which consisted of porridge, followed by bread and butter with marmalade and jam. There was a hash or stew (for which the men in their confined existence had little appetite), although two mornings a week it was replaced by seals' liver, which proved very popular. After prayers at 9.15 am, the men were employed in work parties, maintaining equipment, repairing anything damaged in the winter gales, and clearing away snow from around the ship and huts.

Dinner at 1.00 pm varied daily, with soup followed by seal or tinned meat, and a jam or fruit tart. This was followed by the daily allowance of rum, and smoking was permitted on the mess deck during winter quarters. Another three hours' work in the afternoons preceded supper at 5.00 pm, when some men would have bread and butter with tea, while others would consume the remains of the seal or tinned meats. Afterwards those who had been inside had the opportunity to take some exercise, and the evenings were free for games like whist and chess, and such activities as reading, woodcarving and letter writing. Hammocks were slung at 10.00 pm.

The officers ate at different times from the men, but had the same food. Arrangements were made in the cooks' routines to allow them time to exercise, for otherwise their responsibilities generally would have confined them to the ship.

Each month the doctors Koettlitz and Wilson would note the weight and measurement, and examine the blood, of each person on board, and so keep a record of each man's physical condition throughout the expedition.

On 13 May 1902 the temperature was down to -43 degrees F, but the problems were caused by wind and bad weather, rather than by low temperatures.

Saturdays were devoted to cleaning the ship, while Sundays had inspection, the church service, and a meal of New Zealand mutton while stocks lasted. On 23 June the mess deck was gaily decorated for the mid-winter festival, and the men enjoyed a feast which included turtle soup, mutton and plum pudding, followed by speeches and a sing-song.

Lighting during the winter-time on board was by paraffin lamps, since the windmill (by which they had hoped to have an electricity supply) broke down during a gale on 2 May. The stock of candles was used frugally in order to leave sufficient for a second winter, with the surplus grease being recast and augmented with blubber to further eke out the stock.

The tobacco allowance was one pound per month. As winter came to an end and with the prospect of the sledging season ahead smoking was to be permitted in camp, but not on the march.

A monthly publication, *The South Polar Times*, edited by Shackleton, appeared four times during the winter, with a wide variety of anonymous contributions by officers and men alike. Enhanced by Dr Wilson's fine illustrations, each issue was read avidly.

The large hut was taken over for an entertainment planned after the mid-winter celebrations, consisting of musical items and a comedy. Rehearsals had been conducted amidst much secrecy by Lieutenant Royds, whose daily piano-playing in the *Discovery* was a welcome feature. Edgar illustrated the programmes for the entertainment, which was appreciated by performers and audience alike, in spite of the low temperatures. Later in the winter Royds organised a negro minstrel troupe, for which the seamen went to great lengths to look authentic, even if the sounds were not particularly musical!

The sun re-appeared on 22 August, ending four months of the dark winter. During the next week provisions were weighed out, dog harnesses assembled, and clothing and equipment prepared for the sledging trips planned for the spring. The sledges had been made of ash in Oslo, with elm and maple also used on the sledge runners.

On 10 September Edgar was among six men led by Lieutenant Royds to Black Island. During a gale one of the sleeping bags was blown away — fortunately a single one — and they managed with four people squeezing into one designed for three. Two days later they recovered the missing bag, four miles away. On 2 October almost the identical party went on a three-week journey to Cape Crozier to augment the information left for a relief ship.

During the Antarctic summer of 1902 – 3 the major sledging journey was undertaken by Scott, accompanied by Dr Wilson and Lieutenant Shackleton. They reached what was then the furthest south, latitude 82 degrees 17', and covered 960 statute miles during three months away. But their return journey was precarious, with Shackleton suffering from scurvy and needing to be dragged on the sledge the last stage. Both Scott and Wilson were exhausted by the effects of that journey and the physical work on a limited diet, but they were cheered to find that a relief ship, the *Morning*, had arrived, bringing news of the outside world.

While the three men were away Edgar had accompanied Royds on sledge journeys, until the arrival of the relief ship, whereupon he was occupied in transporting supplies across the ten miles separating the two vessels. The crews would meet half way to transfer supplies, when Edgar's strength would be put to good use. Scott had noted that in any contest among the men involving strength Edgar was invariably the winner.

As there was no sign of the ice breaking up to free the *Discovery,* and the *Morning* would need to depart by mid-February to avoid being similarly trapped in the ice, the company prepared for a second Antarctic winter. This would prove to be substantially colder, although a most valuable time for scientific work.

Against his wishes, Shackleton was invalided home in the *Morning*. What he perceived as his humiliation bred in him a determination to prove his suitability for Antarctic exploration. This he would do in the 1907–9 *Nimrod* expedition, and later demonstrating his leadership qualities after the *Endeavour* was crushed by ice in 1914–15.

As the second winter confinement drew to an end, Scott was already planning another major sledging trip, to explore the polar plateau to the west. The two men accompanying him on this were to figure prominently in the later *Terra Nova* expedition — Edgar Evans and Chief Stoker William Lashly. Unusually for the popular conception of the archetypal seaman, Lashly was a teetotaller and a non-smoker. But such was his strength and character that some to this day feel that his inclusion in the polar party of 1911–12 might have made all the difference.

Initially accompanied by a support party, the three men were away from 12 October for two months, covering 1,100 miles. In many ways this was more of an achievement than the Southern Journey. On the Polar Plateau at an altitude of 9,000 feet they had to contend with dreadful wind conditions. Each man was pulling between 170 to 200 lbs in weight, but Scott wrote that with Edgar and Lashly's strength the sledge became as 'a living thing'.

A blizzard kept them tentbound for several days, when the men shared a three-man sleeping bag. Scott noted that during this time he learned more of life in the lower deck than he had hitherto in his Naval career! In spite of the gulf between officers and men they evidently got on well, agreeing that they could make a better job of running the Royal Navy than the Board of the Admiralty did. With the restricted diet, Edgar's thoughts turned to pork, while Lashly's were of apples.

Making their way back to the ship on 14 December 1903, Edgar and Scott fell the full length of the harness into a crevasse. Fortunately Lashly, who was behind the sledge, managed with difficulty to haul them out. Edgar commented a number of times 'My word, sir, but that was a close call!' They returned to the *Discovery* on Christmas Eve.

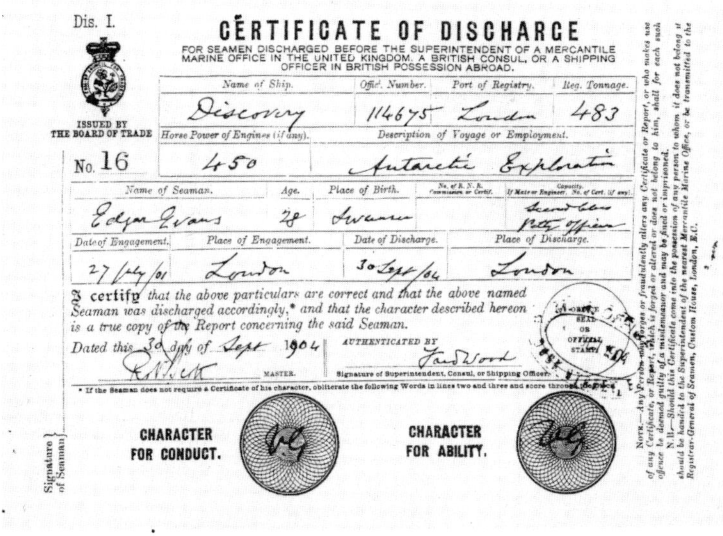
Dis. I.

CERTIFICATE OF DISCHARGE

FOR SEAMEN DISCHARGED BEFORE THE SUPERINTENDENT OF A MERCANTILE MARINE OFFICE IN THE UNITED KINGDOM, A BRITISH CONSUL, OR A SHIPPING OFFICER IN BRITISH POSSESSION ABROAD.

ISSUED BY THE BOARD OF TRADE

No. 16

Name of Ship.	Offl. Number.	Port of Registry.	Reg. Tonnage.
Discovery	114675	London	483

Horse Power of Engines (if any).	Description of Voyage or Employment.
450	Antarctic Exploration

Name of Seaman.	Age.	Place of Birth.	No. of R. N. R. Commission or Certif.	Capacity. If Mate or Engineer, No. of Cert. (if any).
Edgar Evans	28	Swansea		Second Class Petty Officer

Date of Engagement.	Place of Engagement.	Date of Discharge.	Place of Discharge.
27 July/01	London	30 Sept/04	London

I certify that the above particulars are correct and that the above named Seaman was discharged accordingly,* and that the character described hereon is a true copy of the Report concerning the said Seaman.

Dated this 30 day of Sept 1904

MASTER.

AUTHENTICATED BY

Signature of Superintendent, Consul, or Shipping Officer.

SEAL OR OFFICIAL STAMP

* If the Seaman does not require a Certificate of his character, obliterate the following Words in lines two and three and score through the space.

Signature of Seaman

CHARACTER FOR CONDUCT. V.G.

CHARACTER FOR ABILITY. V.G.

NOTE.—Any Person who forges or fraudulently alters any Certificate or Report, or who makes use of any Certificate, or Report, which is forged or altered or does not belong to him, shall for each such offence be deemed guilty of a misdemeanor and may be fined or imprisoned.

N.B.—Should this Certificate come into the possession of any person to whom it does not belong it should be handed to the Superintendent of the nearest Mercantile Marine Office, or be transmitted to the Registrar-General of Seamen, Custom House, London, E.C.

Figure 8. Edgar Evans's discharge certificate, 1904. (Ken Goddard)

Some weeks later the company was surprised to be joined by not one but two relief ships, for the *Morning* was this time accompanied by the old whaler, the *Terra Nova*. After the difficulties with ice the previous year the Admiralty had taken over responsiblity for getting the men back, being prepared to abandon the *Discovery* and bring the men and necessary equipment home in the two relief vessels.

This intervention, and the possibility of being ordered to abandon their ship, was most unwelcome to the company, but they became resigned to it as explosives failed to dislodge the *Discovery*, separated by seventeen miles of ice from open water. Although it was becoming late in the season, in February the ice suddenly began to break up, eventually splitting as easily as if it were paper, so that the vessel could move for the first time in two years.

Returning to Britain in September 1904, the members of the crew were given two months' leave, and the names of Edgar and Lashly were among the six specially commended in Scott's report to the Admiralty.

NOTE

1. After the 1910–13 expedition, William Lashly worked with the Board of Trade in Cardiff, before retiring to Hambledon, Hampshire, where he was a bellringer (6 bells, tenor 10 cwt).

CHAPTER 3

Marriage

Edgar was interviewed by the Swansea newspaper, the *South Wales Daily Post*, prior to returning to London to be paid off. The reporter described him as being 'reticent as to his own deeds and expansive as to the deeds of others'. In speaking of his sledging trip to the west, Edgar said:

> It's an uncanny feeling standing there, surrounded by everlasting snow, gigantic 'nunataks' [peaks of rock projecting above the land ice] all around you, and dead silence which is almost deafening. Not a sign of life, no birds to speak of, only a melancholy seal to look at, and his blessed hide not worth a cent in the European market. Six of us were chosen to do this trip, which was 300 miles from the ship, and lasted nine weeks and three days: but three went back. We saw absolutely nothing. We were 9,200 feet high on the ice-cap, and away towards the Pole was a range of unclimbable mountains. Nobody knows what lies behind it. [1]

Although denying to the reporter a rumour that he might be engaged to a local lady, once he had been discharged from the Expedition in London on 30 September, Edgar was indeed concerned with domestic matters. At the age of twenty-eight he was preparing for marriage to his first cousin, Lois Beynon, daughter of William Beynon, licensee of the 'Ship Inn' at Middleton, and niece of Edgar's mother. Mrs Sarah Evans had herself been the daughter of another William Beynon who had held the licence of the 'Ship'.

Whereas Lois — as well as Edgar — was known to patrons of the 'Ship', she was also well known to a very different section of Gower society — the congregation of St Mary's church at Rhosili. Twenty-five year old Lois had a lovely singing voice, and was a prominent member of the church choir. In former years she had sung at local concerts with the daughters of the previous rector, Revd J. Ponsonby Lucas. [2]

23

Figure 9.   Edgar Evans in 1904. Taken at the time of his marriage, this picture used to hang in Wind Street Post Office, but is now in the Royal Mail premises in Swansea Enterprise Park.   (Royal Mail)

The marriage of a man recently returned from a voyage to the other side of the world, to a local woman well known to churchgoers and patrons of the 'Ship', was worthy of comment in the *South Wales Daily Post*:

Rhosili Wedding

Mr Edgar Evans of the Discovery and Miss Lois Beynon

Rhosili, Gower, was agog with excitement on Tuesday, the occasion being the wedding of Miss Lois Beynon, youngest daughter of Mr William Beynon, of the popular Ship Inn, and Mr Edgar Evans, son of Mr Charles Evans, of Paxton Place, Swansea, who has sprung into prominence by reason of the fact that he was one of the crew of the Discovery sent out for the purpose of Antarctic exploration. The village expressed their well-wishes by firing a feu-de-joie, and Rhosili church, where the marriage ceremony was performed by Rev Lewis Hughes, rector, was filled. The bride, who looked very charming in crepoline silk, trimmed with chiffon, with picture hat to match, and carrying in her hand an ivory-bound prayer book, the gift of the bridegroom, was attended by Miss Gladys Thomas (cousin) and Miss Ida Faull (niece) both of whom looked neat and pretty, and wore dress rings, the gift of the bridegroom. Mr Enoch Beynon (brother of the bride) acted as best man. The service was fully choral, Mrs Henry Richards presiding at the organ. The wedding breakfast was laid at the Ship, and later on the happy pair left for London, amid further firing by coastguardmen, farmers, and others. The presents were many.[3]

Similarly the *Gower Church Magazine* reported in January 1905:

On December 13th a very interesting and pretty wedding took place in Rhosili church. The contracting parties were Miss Lois Beynon, daughter of Mr and Mrs Beynon, of the Ship Inn, Rhosili, and Mr Edgar Evans of Swansea — one of the popular crew of the Discovery, the vessel that returned recently from the expedition to the South Pole. The 'Swansea boy' was one of the two men who accompanied Captain Scott on his perilous journey 270 miles further south than all the rest of the crew.[4] He has seen and experienced much in his distinguished career with Capt. Scott, and has been promoted accordingly in the service of the Navy. He is robust and courageous to a degree, and has during his voyage added much to his previous knowledge and attainments. Like every truly brave man, he is far from being boastful, and requires considerable persuasion to make himself relate anything about himself. When asked by the clergyman to state his rank and profession, he was content to describe himself as a simple mariner. He is therefore one of those who are likely to do great things and make his mark in the World.

His spouse, Miss Lois Beynon, was quite as popular in her own sphere. Possessed of a good voice and fond of singing, she rendered great assistance for years in the services of the Church in Rhosili, and rendered great aid in the local concerts held from time to time in this Parish and the surrounding parishes. Her services were greatly appreciated, as was evidenced in the numerous and costly wedding presents given her by a large number of friends and relatives. The Church was full of interested friends to witness the wedding service, which was fully choral: and we may say the singing was worthy of the bright occasion. The voices in chanting the special psalm and the two well-known hymns were remarkably sweet and one could feel that the hearts of all were full.

Outside also were the usual tokens of rejoicing, several being actively engaged in firing large guns. After the service in church, about fifty sat down to the first breakfast table, when appropriate toasts were given and heartily responded to. Afterwards another large number sat down to breakfast, given at the Picnic Room, which was prettily decorated with ivy and evergreens. About 2 o'clock all assembled to say farewell to the wedded couple on their departure for their honeymoon. They were going to London, and from there to Portsmouth, where Mr. Evans will reside for the next two years. May every blessing follow them in their new home!

Edgar had been promoted to Petty Officer, first class (now termed Chief Petty Officer), backdated to April 1904, and given permission to train as a gunnery instructor at HMS *Excellent*, the Royal Naval Gunnery School at Whale Island, Portsmouth. [5]

For the next five-and-a-half years — the total of their married life together — Edgar and Lois lived in Portsmouth, with Edgar working mainly at HMS *Vernon* after completing his gunnery instructor's training. For Lois

Figure 10. St Mary's church, Rhosili.   (Jane Gregor)

it must have been quite a contrast from rural Gower. They lived at 12 Walden Road in the district of Stamshaw, where their elder son Norman Edgar was born on 18 August 1905, and their daughter Muriel on 9 November of the following year. Afterwards the family moved to 52 Chapel Street in the suburb of Buckland, where Ralph was born on 4 December 1908.[6] Both boys were baptised at Rhosili church during visits to Gower, on 24 December 1905 and 28 August 1910 respectively.

Scott wrote from the Royal Naval Club in Portsmouth on 23 July 1905[7] enquiring about the progress of Edgar's naval career, and saying, 'I shall not get a ship till next year, when I shall be on the look-out for you'. Like the other crew members, Edgar received a complimentary copy of Scott's book *The Voyage of the Discovery*, published in two volumes in October 1905, price two guineas.

Edgar was evidently an effective instructor: his gun crews won the Royal Naval Tattoo for field gunnery at the newly-opened White City in London in 1906, and again the following year. He was remembered as a strict disciplinarian, who gave due credit to hard workers, but had no time for shirkers. He was known in the lower deck as 'Taff' Evans.[8]

Figure 11. Royal naval gun crew, 1907. Edgar Evans is fourth from the right. (SM)

NOTES

1. *SWDP*, 20 September 1904.

2. Robert Lucas, *A Gower Family* (Chippenham, 1986).

3. *SWDP*, 14 December 1904.

4. The mention of Edgar having accompanied Scott 270 miles further south than anyone else is inaccurate — perhaps confusing the western journey, which involved Edgar, with the southern one, which did not.

5. SM: Copy of Certificate of Service, June 1962.

6. The Superintendent Registrar, Portsmouth. Mr Ray Bourton kindly obtained copies of the birth certificates.

7. Scott Polar Research Institute (henceforth SPRI): Sotheby's catalogue 7 December 1984.

8. SM: Article by N. Webb of the Shiplovers' Society, n.d.

CHAPTER 4

The *Terra Nova*

Meanwhile, on the other side of the world, Shackleton, who had been invalided home in the *Morning* in 1903 after the southern journey with Scott and Wilson, led his own Antarctic expedition in 1907 in the *Nimrod*. This established the Magnetic South Pole, achieved the first ascent of a polar mountain, and forged a route (named the Beardmore Glacier by Shackleton, after his principal backer) on to the polar plateau. Shackleton turned back ninety-seven miles from the Pole itself, commenting that his wife would prefer to have a live donkey than a dead lion.

On his return to Britain in June 1909, Shackleton received a hero's welcome, and a knighthood. This extrovert Irishman basked in the public acclaim, which by comparison was anathema to the more reserved Scott. Shackleton's achievements spurred Scott into planning another Antarctic expedition, to follow up the scientific work commenced in the *Discovery*, and to attain the South Pole for the British Empire.

Unlike in 1901, there was now no financial backing from any scientific or learned society, so it was necessary to launch a public appeal for funds, and Scott embarked on generating interest among the business communities of the major cities. He was assisted in this by Lieutenant 'Teddy' Evans, formerly second officer of the relief ship, the *Morning*. Evans had abandoned his own plans of leading an Antarctic expedition, to become Scott's second in command. Lieutenant Evans thrived on public relations work, and built up good contacts in Cardiff (from where his own grandfather came), particularly with Daniel Radcliffe of the shipping and coal firm, Evan Thomas Radcliffe. [1]

The proposed British Antarctic Expedition, as it was known, aroused immense public interest, if not exactly in funding it, for almost 8,000 applied to join. Preference was given to those with Antarctic experience, and to members of the Royal Navy for the crew. Dr Edward Wilson was appointed chief of scientific staff, and he selected his team from throughout the British Empire. Like Shackelton in 1907, to help with funds Scott decided to take two paying volunteers. He also took three motorised sledges, for Shackleton had used an Arrol-Johnson motor vehicle in the *Nimrod* expedition.

Scott wrote on 23 March 1910 telling Edgar that he had applied for his services on the proposed expedition, and saying, 'I expect you will be appointed in about a fortnight's time, and I shall want you at the ship to help fitting her out'. [2]

The *Discovery* had been sold to the Hudson's Bay Company and was not available, but the expedition obtained the *Terra Nova*, one of the relief vessels in 1904 when the *Discovery* had been locked in the ice. Built by Alexander Stephens and Sons in Dundee in 1884, with a length of 187 feet and tonnage 749, the *Terra Nova* was the largest whaling ship afloat, and had auxiliary steam power. She was fitted out in London's West India Docks, and re-rigged as a barque. The length of the *Terra Nova* was approximately three fifths that of Brunel's SS *Great Britain*, now back in Bristol.

Publicising the expedition to raise funds was made more difficult by the death of King Edward VII, and by a general election, but eventually Scott could announce that the expedition would depart in June 1910. Cardiff was to be the port of departure since, through the contacts of Lieutenant Evans and the efforts of Mr Daniel Radcliffe, its citizens had provided the largest financial assistance of any city.

While the ship was being fitted out in the West India docks, Edgar worked at 36–38 Victoria Street, the rented London office which served as the expedition headquarters. Seeing Edgar, Australian geologist Griffith Taylor commented, 'His size and strength made me incite Wright [Canadian physicist Charles Wright] to show some of the scientists could at any rate "Walk" — so we did the standard 50 miles [from Brighton] to London in twenty-four hours'. [3]

Before joining the ship at Cardiff, Edgar went to Gower, to visit his widowed mother (Charles Evans had died in 1907), then living with her sister Mrs Powell in Pitton, [4] before walking the sixteen miles towards

Swansea to see his elder brother Charles at Cwm Farm, Sketty. Years later one of his nieces[5] recalled that her uncle took her up in his arms and promised that he would come and see her when he returned from the Antarctic: that promise he was unable to keep. Edgar's family stayed at Falmouth House in Clydach Road, Morriston, on the northern side of Swansea, at the home of Lois's elder sister Beatrice, who was married to iron merchant, John Faull.

In Cardiff, the *Terra Nova* received free docking facilities and a hundred tons of steam coal. The officers were invited by the Cardiff Chamber of Commerce to a farewell banquet at the Royal Hotel on Monday, 13 June: the crew were entertained nearby at Barry's Hotel.

After the meal, Scott summoned the men to join them for a smoking concert where Edgar, being from south Wales, was seated between Captain Scott and the Lord Mayor of Cardiff. When the flag of the city was presented to the Expedition, Edgar rose to his feet and delivered an impromptu speech, as reported by The *Cambrian*:[6]

EDGAR EVANS'S CARDIFF SPEECH
Abertawe Boy who is Southward Bound
Breezy Speech at Cardiff Banquet

Captain Scott, C.V.O., and the officers of the British Antarctic Expedition vessel, Terra Nova, were entertained to dinner at Cardiff on Monday evening by the commercial community, the President of the Cardiff Chamber of Commerce in the chair. The crew were also entertained to dinner and £1,000 for the funds of the Expedition were collected at the former ceremony, at which an event of special interest to Swansea also occurred, when the Lord Mayor presented to the Expedition a banner emblazoned with the arms of Cardiff.

Chief Seaman Edgar Evans, of Swansea, one of the biggest and burliest members of the crew, was received with three times three as he rose from his seat between the Lord Mayor and Captain Scott. With the typical modesty of a Jack Tar, and with an unmistakable West Wales accent, he said:

I think it's out of place for me to sit up here with Captain Scott, but, like Lord Charles Beresford, whatever I have to say I'll say it in as few words as possible. (cheers)

Every man in the ship has confidence in Captain Scott. I know him well and he knows me very well — (laughter) — and I know Lieutenant Evans very well. (cheers)

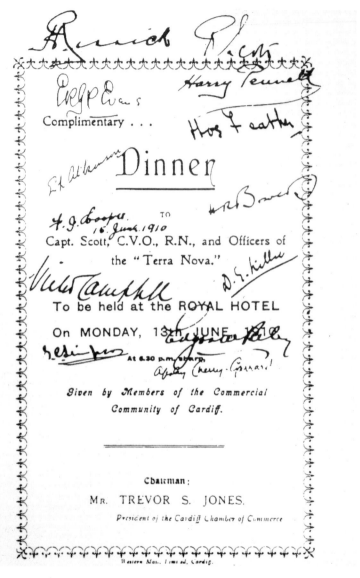

Figure 12.   Menu from the farewell banquet at the Royal Hotel, Cardiff, 13 June 1910.
(Captain Scott Society)

Every man in this Expedition is heart and soul in the business, and as it has got to be a success this time — (cheers) — every man will do his best.

As a representative of Wales I am pleased to meet you all, but whether Wales or Ireland, if Captain Scott had only said he was going again I would go too. (cheers) No one else would have induced me to go there again, but if there is a man in the world who will bring this to a successful issue, Captain Scott is the man. (renewed cheers)

As regards the flag, if Captain Scott wants to know the English translation of the Welsh mottoes, here it is: 'Awake, it is day' and 'The Welsh dragon leads the van'.[7]

The crew appreciate what you have done for them. I hope we shall all meet again — and we shall. (Cheers) Of course, that depends on Captain Scott bringing back the Pole. (loud laughter) We cannot put it into the museum, but if we do bring it back I hope you will let it go to Swansea. (loud cheers and laughter)

Everyone has every confidence in Captain Scott and Lieut. Evans, and if we ever do come back we hope to meet you in Cardiff again. (loud cheers)

Mr. Evans's Swansea Connections

Chief Seaman Evans, although a Swansea boy, makes his home at Portsmouth, but he was born at Abertawe, and his father, Mr. Charles Evans, sailed out of Swansea in the Glasgow trade for years. He married a daughter of Mr. W. Beynon of Rhossilly, and a brother-in-law is Mr. Jno. Faull, iron merchant, Clydach Road, Morriston. A brother is Mr. Charles Evans, farmer, Singleton. His mother still lives in Gower, and during the 15 years he has been in the Navy he has visited every quarter of the globe. He is 35 years of age, three children in family, and expects to be away at least four years.[8]

After leaving the hotel, it seems that there was some boisterous behaviour, with some of the crew the worse for wear for drink. It took six men to help Edgar to re-embark, although this was because of his size and condition rather than any aggressive manner.

Another of Edgar's nieces, twenty-two year-old Sarah Evans, went on board the *Terra Nova*, which was open to visitors while docked in Cardiff. Her uncle introduced her to Captain Scott, who gave her a biscuit of the sledging rations.[9] On Wednesday, 15 June, she was in one of the pleasure steamers which accompanied the *Terra Nova* out of Cardiff Docks as far as Penarth Head, as the ship made her way down the Bristol Channel. On the Gower cliffs at Rhosili other members of the family watched the ship make her way towards the open sea: the expedition which was to become an epic in British exploration was underway.

Initially the *Terra Nova* sailed without Captain Scott, who was busy raising funds. He was to sail by the tramp steamer *Saxon* to join the company in Cape Town. Under the command of Lieutenant 'Teddy' Evans, the *Terra Nova* sailed to Madeira, where the stop at Funchal enabled one co-opted member of the crew, Captain Lawrence Oates, to visit his father's grave. Oates was one of the two volunteers on board, each of whom had paid £1,000 for the privilege. A thirty year-old cavalry officer with the 6th Royal Inniskilling Dragoons, Oates had served with distinction in South Africa during the Anglo-Boer War. During an enemy engagement in the eastern Cape on 6 March 1901, he had received a thigh wound and been invalided home. His courage and leadership on that occasion earned him the epithet 'Never-say-die Oates'. A member of the landed gentry, with his home at Gestingthorpe Hall in rural Essex, he was one of the first men in the country to own a motor-cycle.

His arrival at the West India Docks, dressed in an old raincoat, had aroused the comment from Petty Officer Thomas Crean that they 'never for a moment thought he was an officer, for they were usually so smart. We made up our minds he was a farmer, he was... so nice and friendly, just like one of ourselves, but oh! he was a gentleman, quite a gentleman, and always a gentleman!'

However, Oates's success at fitting in with the sailors was counter-productive, as he was taken on the voyage from Cardiff. Being a cavalry officer and with extensive experience of horses, his expertise might have been better employed travelling overland through Europe to choose suitable Siberian ponies for the expedition: the choices made by others less well-equipped to do so left much to be desired.

The other volunteer was Apsley Cherry-Garrard, recently graduated from Oxford, where he had rowed in a winning eight at Henley Regatta. Appointed as assistant zoologist, he would later write the definitive account of the expedition, entitled *The Worst Journey in the World*.

The *Terra Nova* was found to be sluggish, and heavy on coal. In fact, when needed as a relief ship in 1904 she had been towed by a relay of cruisers speedily through the Mediterranean and the Suez Canal. Edgar wrote to his mother before they reached Madeira: [10]

S Yacht Terra Nova
At sea
21 June 1910

Dear Mother,

A few lines to let you know that I am in the best of health and I hope this will
find you the same. We are at sea bound for Madeira and I am quite sure that I
shall not have time to write to you from there, as we shall be far too busy. We
have had very fair weather so far but the winds have not been favourable so we
shall not get into Madeira on the day we ought to. I expect we shall arrive there
on the 24th and leave on the 27th but that's not certain yet. The programme may
be altered at any time. The ship is very much like the *Discovery* but a good deal
older. I expected Charley, Mary Ann and Will Thomas up to Cardiff but they
did not come. I saw Annie, Sarah and Sally there, they are all quite well and
wished to be remembered to you, Dear Mother. I will write to you again from
Cape Town and I should very much like to hear from you there. My address will
be

Edgar Evans
S Yacht Terra Nova
Cape Town
South Africa

You will have to hurry up if you are going to write from there as we leave on
the 1st of August for Australia. Please remember me to all the Aunts and Uncles
and anyone that inquires. I have no more to say at present so will close with
fondest love and best wishes. I am your Everloving Son

Edgar xxxx

The following day he wrote to his sister-in-law and her husband, John
and Beatrice Faull, of Falmouth House, Morriston, saying: [11]

The winds have been against us nearly the whole of the time. I suppose we shall
get a fair wind some time. It's a good job we have had some decent weather so
as to get things a bit square. We were in a bad state when we left Cardiff. I'm
happy to tell you that the leak is as bad as ever, but it may close up in time. I
will send you a programme of our movements from Cape Town if I can get any
reliable information.

On 15 July they celebrated crossing the line [the Equator], with Edgar
presiding as Neptune. After passing the uninhabited island of South
Trinidad, they stopped off at Simonstown, just south of Cape Town, from
where Edgar wrote to his mother. [12]

Terra Nova
Cape Town
South Africa
17th August, 1910

My dear Mother,

I received your most welcome letter yesterday, glad to learn that you were in good health and to let you know that I am the same. We arrived here on the 15th, on the whole the voyage from Madeira was a good one, but for the last 14 days the weather was pretty bad, plenty of wind and a very heavy sea, we were 15 days overdue but that was principally because we had no wind earlier in the trip. It's 10 years since I was at this place and the place has not altered but very little. We are not really at Cape Town but at Simons Bay — it's 22 miles away, and it's the Naval base, at present we are refitting the ship and repairing some trifling damage. The mail only leaves here once a week and that's a bit awkward, because you have to wait if you miss it: one left here today but I failed to catch it.

Dear Mother, according to the programme we leave here for Melbourne but I don't think we shall go, I rather think we shall go straight on to Lyttleton as we are a little late. As far as we know we shall leave for the ice early in December, but I will let you know about that later on. I was rather surprised to learn that Aunt Ann was in Swansea. She told me she did not expect she should ever go there again. I had a letter from Charlie today — quite a spasm for him wasn't it?

There is nothing of importance to tell you this time, Capt'n Scott is at Pretoria but comes here on the 20th then goes on to New Zealand. I will close now, with fondest love and best wishes,

I am your everloving Son,
    Edgar xxxx
(Regards to all the relations)

Scott rejoined them after fundraising in Pretoria, and decided to take over command of the vessel from Lieutenant Evans, and send Dr Wilson on to New Zealand with the wives of the three officers. Contrary to what Edgar had expected, the *Terra Nova* managed to stop off in Melbourne on 12 October. It was there that Scott received the fateful telegram:

'Madeira. Am going south — Amundsen.'

Previously the Norwegian's plans were to reach the North Pole, but that had been attained by the American Robert Peary the previous year. So, without notifying his backers until he had left Madeira and was beyond contact with the outside world, Roald Amundsen turned Nansen's ship, the *Fram,* towards Antarctic waters. To his credit, Scott determined not to alter his own plans, and declined to be drawn into any 'race for the Pole'.

Like the *Discovery* in 1901 and the *Nimrod* in 1907, the *Terra Nova* spent a month at Port Lyttleton in New Zealand, where the stores were unloaded and repacked, being marked with a red band for the Main Party, and a green band for the Eastern Party. On the quayside there was practice in assembling the two prefabricated huts, while some repairs were made to the ship. The nineteen ponies and thirty-three dogs were quarantined on Quail Island, [13] before being taken on board once their stables were constructed.

The men's space was on the main deck from the fore hatch to the stem, and Edgar was spokesman in requesting that their comfort be disregarded because of the need to accommodate extra supplies, a gesture which Scott much appreciated.

The members of the crew enjoyed the lavish New Zealand hospitality, and, as Edgar had an abundant fund of anecdotes, one would surmise that he attracted the attention of many persons eager to hear him recount exploits from the *Discovery* days.

The six remaining scientific members joined the expedition, and the vessel was due to sail at 3pm on Saturday 26 November. But on attempting to re-embark Edgar fell in the water, due to intoxication, and Scott dismissed him from the expedition, so that the *Terra Nova* sailed without him. Fortunately for Edgar, she had one more port of call in New Zealand before sailing south, and she had also left behind Scott, who had expedition business with the shipping agents Kinsey and Co. at Christchurch, and who intended to travel overland with Wilson to rejoin his ship.

Edgar approached Scott and asked to be given another chance. At first this was refused, but he persisted and Scott relented, so that they travelled together by express train on Monday, 28 November to Port Chalmers, where the ship had arrived the previous night. Scott noted that 'Evans behaved as if nothing had happened', but we may conclude that Edgar was man enough to admit his fault in asking to be reinstated.

But Lieutenant Evans was displeased to see the petty officer embarking at Port Chalmers, and felt that this was bad for morale. Friction had earlier occurred between the two men when Edgar had pointed out to Captain Scott faults on skis sent from Norway: as a result he had been put in charge of the equipment in place of 'Teddy' Evans. Perhaps there was a clash of personalities, as both the officer and the seaman were outgoing, gregarious persons, who functioned best in their separate spheres.

With 462 tons of coal on board, the *Terra Nova* sailed from Port Chalmers at 2.30 pm on Tuesday, 29 November 1910, followed by many small craft filled with well-wishers seeing them off. For five of those sixty-five on board it was to be their last glimpse of a flower, a tree or a woman.

Compared with the crossing in 1901, they had a most hazardous time within a week of leaving New Zealand. On 2 December the *Terra Nova* encountered a fierce storm, causing cases to break loose on the upper deck. With heavy seas breaking over the ship attempts were made to re-lash the cargo, and to jettison many of the thirty tons of coal in sacks along with other deck cargo. When the pumps became choked there was real danger of losing the heavily-laden ship. It took a night and a day of frantic baling out — officers and men alike operating in relays — along with desperate work in filthy conditions to clear the pumps, to put matters right. The casualties were two horses and one of the dogs. Afterwards the men had to cope with dirt from the stables leaking onto their hammocks and bedding, while everyone attempted to dry out.

The pack-ice was encountered further north than anticipated, and it took twenty days to get through, which caused Scott much alarm because of the large amount of coal consumed during a time of slow progess.

On Christmas Day there was full attendance at the Service taken by Scott, where he noted a 'lusty singing of the hymns'. The men's dinner was at midday, with beer and whisky, while that of the officers was at 6.00 pm, accompanied by champagne, port and liqueurs. Five days later the *Terra Nova* at last got out of the pack ice into open sea.

NOTES

1. Anthony Johnson, 'Scott of the Antarctic and Cardiff', *Morgannwg*, xxvi (1982) and xxvii (1983).

2. SPRI: Sotheby's catalogue 7 December 1984.

3. SM: letter to Stanley Richards, 11 June 1962.

4. *CDL*, 13 February 1913. Brian Lile supplied the date of Charles Evans's death.

5. Recollection of Mrs E. Young on 21 July 1993. I am obliged to Bill Young for bringing his mother to Swansea Museum.

6. *The Cambrian*, 17 June 1910.

7. In Welsh the mottoes are 'Deffro, mae'n ddydd', and 'Y ddraig goch a ddyry gychwyn'. Edgar was not a Welsh speaker, although he spoke the English Gower dialect (SM: letter from Mrs Sarah Owen, 8 March 1962).

8. Abertawe is, of course, the Welsh name for Swansea. Edgar's age at that time was not thirty-five but thirty-four. The final statement about being away for at least four years is incorrect: sixteen months later Captain Scott was to write to Mrs Lois Evans when it became evident that they would be away for a third year.

9. Gwent Jones, 'Edgar Evans: A Gower Hero', *Gower*, vii (1955). Scott Gregson informs me that the biscuit was not consumed.

10. Letter at SM.

11. SPRI: Sotheby's catalogue, 7 December 1984.

12. The property of Miss Sarah Evans.

13. Photograph at the Oates Museum, Gilbert White's House, Selborne.

CHAPTER 5

Antarctica, 1911

Unable to land at Cape Crozier because of the swell, the *Terra Nova* dropped anchor at what was renamed Cape Evans (after Lieutenant Evans) beneath the volcanic Mount Erebus. Edgar described the crossing in his final letter to his mother: [1]

3 January, 1911

My dear Mother,

A few lines to let you know that we have arrived here safely after rather a long voyage.

Since leaving New Zealand we have had some pretty bad weather, which did some damage to the ship and was also the cause of two ponies and one dog dying, but we got over that allright.

After we got to the ice we had a job to get through it—it was so thick at times we were completely blocked by it; it took us 19 days to get through 370 miles of it, the conditions were more severe than when I was down here before in the "Discovery", but there is one thing, nothing seems so strange now as it did then, in fact the place looks quite familiar to me.

Our programme is the main party is going to winter at Cape Crozier that is 70 miles from where the Discovery wintered and a small party will go to King Edward land to winter and to survey that place (I belong to the main party); in all probability we shall start sledging in 3 weeks time, but it will only be to lay down Depots for the long journey which will take place about next October: then the dash for the South Pole will be made and we hope to be successful.

It all depends on how we get on the first year as to how long we stay here but we hope only to be here about 15 months. After the ship has landed the parties she will go back to New Zealand and stay over the winter, coming down to us next December and I hope to have a letter from you then, I wrote to you all the way out but I have had only one letter from you. I will send address and if you write in August it will catch the ship coming down here.

I am pleased to tell you dear mother that I am in the best of health and I hope this will find you the same.

The stamp which is on this letter is an Antarctic stamp, so you must keep it, it is marked 'Victoria Land' and quite unique, rather a curiosity.

I suppose you saw plenty of Lois and the children while they were home — I expect Lois had a job to get them back to school when she got back. I expect it is a bit cold with you now it is the New Year. I must wish you a happy one tho you will be a long time getting this letter. Please remember me to all at Pitton and all relations who inquire for me.

Well dear mother I don't think I have any more to tell you at present so I will draw to a close; we are very busy getting Provisions etc out of the ship,

With love and best wishes to all,
I am your Everloving Son

Edgar. xxxx

My address will be Edgar Evans, British Antarctic
Expedition, c/o Messrs Kinsey & Co., Christchurch, New Zealand.

That phrase 'but we got over it allright' (after the mention of their sea crossing) is typical of Edgar, never one to complain about difficult situations. He would make light of what Shakespeare described as 'the slings and arrows of outrageous fortune',[2] seeking to face life's problems square on, and striving to overcome each hurdle, rather than bewailing his lot.

The equipment was unloaded, with the men working from 5.00 am to 10.00 pm for more than a week, and the dogs were put to good use transporting supplies one-and-a-half miles across the ice to the site of their camp. During this time Scott commented: 'Evans shows himself wonderfully capable, and I haven't a doubt as to the working of the sledges he has fitted up.'

Unfortunately, on 8 January 1911, one of the three motor tractors fell through the ice while being unloaded and sank: that was £1,000 worth of machinery lost — representing a year's salary for Scott, or two years' salary for Wilson, or the contribution from Oates or Cherry-Garrard.[3]

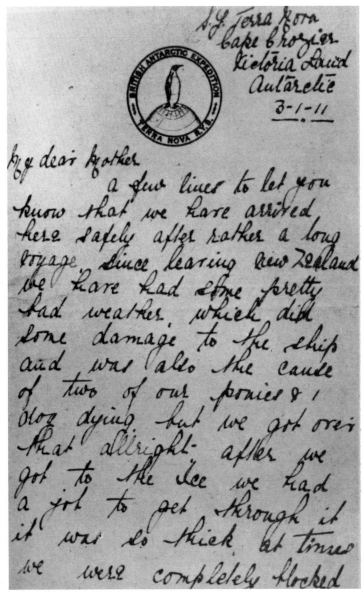

Figure 13. The first page of Edgar Evans's last letter to his mother. (SM)

After the unloading, Edgar was landed further up the coast to look after three young scientists on a geological expedition in the western mountains. These were the Australian geologists Griffith Taylor and Frank Debenham, and Canadian physicist Charles Wright. Initially the four took two sledges (each man pulling a weight of about 270 lbs), but they would be laying a depot of supplies, and proceeding with one sledge for much of the time.

With his experience from the *Discovery* expedition, Edgar's task was to teach the three how to cook and camp in those conditions. For the first week he was cook, with Debenham being cook's mate and taking over for the second week. Wright would then become cook's mate, with Taylor in turn taking over after his week. Among the entries in his Navigating Officer's notebook[4] about that journey, Edgar commented:

> *27 Jan 1911:* Western Sledge Trip—left ship 4.30. Placed depot for Debenham. Proceeded over sea ice towards right side of Glacier. 8 o'clock camped. Watched ship go out of sight. Change. Pemmican & cocoa, not very palatable. Temp +13.

[At the outset of sledging journeys the pemmican was often found to be too rich and abundant, but travellers very soon worked up an appetite for it.]

> *28 Jan:* turned out 8am fairly warm… lunched at 2.30 pm and camped. Scientists and myself examining hills on north side of glacier, came across several batches of Emperor penguins, killed one to take on to depot A. All penguins are moulting. Temp +13.

> *29 Jan:* Got up at 8 o'clock, breakfast, packed sledges and got away. Very heavy going across crushed snow. Lunched at 1.30. During the day several times sledges capsized. Have done about 8 miles nearly at foot of glacier. Very low clouds hanging over the valley, appears to have been a very heavy fall of snow and there is a broken surface. Makes one sweat. Camped at 7pm. Temp +15 about 500 ft above sea level.

[One of them remarked that with the sledge rolling about on the slippery surface they had the appearance of being drunk, but without any of the pleasure of it!]

> *4 Feb:* did not expect to see scenery like this.

> *5 Feb:* passed a good number of seals, all decomposed, that proves the place was once glaciated. Lunched at 1pm. Biscuit and chocolate not filling enough— I'm still very hungry… it's rather hard to believe that the seals climbed all this way up from the sea, but I suppose they must have done so. The majority of

them are crabeaters — I suppose they died of starvation, couldn't find the way down again or there is another theory that they came inland to die, but I can't believe that.

6 Feb: the more one sees of this place the more one is impressed with the rugged scenery, there are mountains all around with glaciers coming down the sides of them, then the valley is extremely interesting from a geological point of view. There are six inland lakes. Of course at present they are frozen over, but in summer they are not. They are made from the thaw of the glaciers melting the snow, some are quite two miles square, and there is any quantity of rocks of all descriptions. I'm getting quite well up in the names of different rocks.

We all got back to camp about 6.30 to the noble feed of biscuits and cheese, my belly fairly rumbles — we hope to get back to glacier camp tomorrow, a feed of pemmican will be very welcome, or anything hot in fact. 4 days of dried biscuits is enough for a while.

7 Feb: we passed the skeleton of an Adelie penguin today, the only one we have seen in the whole of the valley. It's strange, seeing there are so many seal carcasses about, I suppose he got lost.

[All had brought reading matter along, but evidently Wright and Griffith Taylor set aside their choices of German books in favour of Edgar's less demanding selection of *The Red Magazine* and a William Le Queux thriller, which were popular with all of them.]

10 Feb: tried a new experiment, sleeping head & tails, it did not pan out very well.

11 Feb: the penguin that we depoted here has been eaten by Skua gulls, personally I'm not sorry.

14 Feb: last night was the coldest we have had yet. Today has been a very hard day, there have been plenty of prayers offered up.

15 Feb: we lost an ice axe today, going to have a look for it tomorrow, drew lots who should go, my luck.

[Edgar recovered it the following day.]

18 Feb: had a good feed of seals liver for lunch today. We got a new cook today — Taylor not up to the mark yet.

20 Feb: we have decided to push on towards the Koellitz glacier, but are going to try a route close to Brown Island... it now came on to snow and we could not see where we were going, but we had to push on — it's the most damnable surface I have ever seen, I've used up all my good selection of swear words today.

[But there were lighter moments, for later:]

> I've been teaching my comrades how to do fancy knots, and won three dinners
> in bets on a clove hitch with one hand. I've won quite a lot of dinners this trip.

[At a midday lunch break Edgar offered to show his companions how to do a one-handed Clove-hitch. He bet them the price of a dinner (1s. 3d.) that they couldn't do it after seeing him show them six times. Debenham took him on, and much to their surprise he suceeded. Edgar did not turn a hair, but calmly noted the bets that followed. Debenham tried again, and failed, as did Wright and Taylor also. Edgar said he had never seen anyone manage it on their first attempt before, and he later showed them the trick involved.]

> *24 Feb:* tonight we had a game of cards — Australia v Canada & Wales — they
> lost handsomely, as they did last week. I expect they will be after our blood
> soon again.

> *26 Feb:* seen several Skua gulls — didn't expect to find them so far down as
> this... I expect it will get worse each day now that the sun is going down N. Last
> night was the coldest yet, it's pretty chilly now. Temp +5 and has not been much
> higher all day. Great debate tonight, not much in it though. Temp +4.

> *27 Feb:* we passed a glacier on the way which convinced us that all the Maranic
> ranges were sometime glaciers. We went up a deep ravine, about 7 miles long
> which has been cut by the flow of water down from the Glaciers. It all flows
> down towards the mouth of the Koellitz. The gorge opened out into lakes about
> a mile long, with running water going from one into the other and then down the
> gorge seawards... we found plenty of interest during the day... we found a flow
> of lava coming down the mountainside, the first we have seen, and also the
> glaciers are of such a peculiar shape, at one time the whole of this country in the
> lowlands was covered in ice. We got some particularly good views of crystals.
> 1100 ft above sea level. I got a frostbitten ear, through having only my Tam o
> Shanter on, pure carelessness on my part.

> *1 March:* I won a dinner from Deb yesterday, and another from Wright today. I
> also lost one to Taylor the day before. Temperature zero.

> *3 March:* it came on to snow, and very thick but we got along all right. Played
> cards tonight — bridge: W & D played T & I [Wright and Debenham against
> Taylor and Edgar]. We mopped them up handsomely.

> *9 March:* a beautiful morning with a slight wind from the S.E. I think it's the
> first time I have ever spent my birthday sledging, and it promises to be a heavy
> day for us. We got away after breakfast with the small sledge. We celebrated the
> occasion by my having 2 cups of tea and an extra biscuit.

> Tonight we celebrate the occasion by scoffing 1lb of fancy chocolates which we
> brought from the hut and I expect a glorious feed as well.
>
> My companions say sledging is not so nice as it was — I cheer them up by
> saying it's nothing to what spring sledging is, and it isn't. We have had
> remarkably good weather, all except the last week which has been a series of
> disappointments — hope this won't last long.
>
> I feel a bit anxious about the S [Southern] party.'

His final remark in the Navigating Officer's notebook turned out to be
well-founded.

Griffith Taylor later commented:[5] 'It was very thoughtful of Scott to
make Evans the fourth member of my first job... with his previous
Antarctic experience he was very valuable, for the other three were tyroes'.
Frank Debenham, first professor of Geography at Cambridge University,
and founder-director of the Scott Polar Research Institute, described Edgar
as 'A first-rate sledging companion'. He said, 'Taff was wonderful
company, always cheerful and with a great fund of anecdotes. Even in our
arguments over scientific matters he would break in with the most fearful
and wonderful suggestions to send us into fits of laughter'. Debenham
added, 'We got into one or two tight spots on that journey, but he [Edgar]
never showed any alarm and usually made a light joke in the middle of
what looked like being a very risky job'.[6]

Edgar wore a huge Canary Islands hat during the first few sunny days,
but soon turned to the regulation balaclava. He won numerous minor bets
with his one-handed clove-hitch. Glaciers were named after the three
scientists, while Edgar gave the name the Wales Glacier to a tributary in the
northeast corner of the Kukri Hills. He was particularly cautious as they
approached Hut Point, aware of the fate of Seaman Vince nine years
earlier.

Meanwhile Scott had led a thirteen-man depot-laying party to place a
large food depot on the 79th parallel, in order to assist the major southern
journey planned for the following season. There were problems with
weather and ponies, so that the depot was eventually laid at 79 degrees
29'S. This was further north than they had planned, and its position was to
be crucial for at least three members of the Polar Party. Because of the
quantity of supplies it was named One Ton Depot, and laid on 17 February:
on that day exactly a year later the Polar Party would suffer its first

casualty. This depot laying party met up with the geological party at the old *Discovery* hut in March 1911, and waited for the sea to freeze over for them to return by a direct route to the Cape Evans base.

The *Terra Nova*, under the command of Lieutenant Pennell, was due to leave a party of six men under Lieutenant Campbell further east, to be engaged on separate work. The vessel would then winter in New Zealand, returning the following January to collect Campbell's party and then the main party from the base camp. But the vessel made an unexpected return to Cape Evans with the news that the *Fram* was anchored in the Bay of Whales. They had made contact with the Norwegians, and had been impressed with their single-minded efficiency (Amundsen was intent only on reaching the Pole, without the distraction of any scientific progamme). Amundsen had noticed that an ice-flow noted by Shackleton in 1907 had retained its position for a hundred years, and he reasoned that it should thus be stable enough for his own base camp. A base at the eastern end of the Great Ice Barrier meant that the Norwegians could start from fifty miles nearer the Pole than the British party. It also meant that Campbell's Eastern Party had to land elsewhere, and they were landed at Cape Adare, becoming in effect the Northern Party. They would eventually undergo an experience as heroic as that of the Polar party or the Winter Journey, although less well known. Running alarmingly low on coal, the *Terra Nova* then made straight for Port Lyttleton.

On 23 April the sun disappeared below the horizon, and would not be seen again for four months. While there was sufficient light the men would play football on the ice. Edgar was always first choice for the team of Captain Oates, whose instruction 'Go, on, Taff, break them up!' brought the response 'Right 'o, sir', as each game got under way. Scott was less enthusiastic about the football games when Lieutenant Atkinson was laid up through injury.

To reach the South Pole would involve marching a distance of nine hundred miles, roughly equivalent to walking from Land's End to John O'Groats (and the same distance back), carrying food, fuel for cooking and lighting, and camping equipment. The men chosen would traverse much unknown territory, over surfaces ranging from hard slippery ice to those resembling a recently ploughed field. They could expect to encounter steep gradients and to face strong winds and extremely low temperatures; at times each man would be pulling a weight of between 170 and 200 lbs on the sledge.

Figure 14.   The Terra Nova *in Antarctica.*   (Popperfoto)

Scott's own experience on his 1902 southern journey with Wilson and Shackleton, together with Shackleton's 1908 journey on to the Polar plateau (of which Scott had an account), demonstrated that there was no margin for error on a lengthy Antarctic journey. Dogs, ponies and the two motor tractors would be used to move supplies across the Great Ice Barrier — approximately 430 miles. Then Scott aimed to ascend the Beardmore Glacier (about 130 miles), and take to the South Pole a party of four men, who would be assisted by two support parties, which would turn back after laying depots along the route to provision the return.

The winter of 1911 in the 50 by 25 foot pre-fabricated hut at Cape Evans was no idle time for the twenty-five men. Besides the scientific work, the dogs and horses needed exercising (the latter under the supervision of Oates), there were regular duties to be carried out, and the preparation of stores and equipment for the Southern Journey. Photographs show Edgar along with Irish P.O. Thomas Crean mending the reindeer-skin sleeping bags in the hut, and exercising ponies.

On 4 July Surgeon Lieutenant Atkinson, a parasitologist, left the hut to investigate the parasites of fish. A blizzard sprung up, and when he did not swiftly return Edgar called Tom Crean, and the two seamen went out to look for him. When they returned without Atkinson, Scott organised search parties to go in each direction from the hut, with Edgar put in charge of the first of these. Atkinson was eventually found with a badly frostbitten hand, having been out for five hours. During the blizzard he had become disorientated and wandered about for some time. A photograph taken the following day shows Edgar bandaging the officer's hand: Edgar Evans was ever in the forefront of activities.

It was not known then who would comprise the Polar party, but photographer Herbert Ponting wrote:

> In the mess deck Petty Officer Evans was the dominant personality. His previous polar experience, his splendid build, and his stentorian voice and manner of using it, all compelled the respect due to one who would have been conspicuous in any company. He also was one of the leader's towers of strength.... Nobody ever doubted, all through that winter, that Petty Officer Evans would be one of the ones chosen for the Pole.... The party selected by Captain Scott for the Pole journey were the four men who possessed the most striking personalities.

On 2 August Dr Wilson, Lieutenant Bowers and Cherry-Garrard returned from a five week journey to the Emperor Penguin rookery at Cape

Crozier, having obtained three penguin eggs. To advance scientific
knowledge they had accomplished the first Antarctic winter journey,
pulling two sledges in total darkness for much of the time, and enduring
temperatures as low as minus 77 degrees Fahrenheit. The title of Cherry-
Garrard's later book about the entire expedition was chosen by his
publishers, but *The Worst Journey in the World* could have been an apt
description of what those three men experienced. Eight months later two of
them were to die beside Scott.

After the sun had returned on 23 August, Scott took Edgar, along with
Lieutenant Bowers and Raymond Priestley, one of the geologists, on a short
sledging trip to the Ferrar glacier in mid September. He commented, 'The
greatest source of pleasure to me is to realise that I have such men as
Bowers and P.O. Evans for the Southern journey. I do not think that harder
men or better sledge travellers ever took the trail'. In his journal on 11
October Scott noted,

> Edgar Evans has proved a useful member of our party: he looks after our sledges
> and sledge equipment with a care of management and a fertility of resource
> which is wholly astonishing — on 'trek' he is just as sound and hard as ever and
> has an inexhaustible store of anecdote.

Scott judged that he could not commence the Southern Journey before
the end of October, since the ponies would be unable to withstand the low
temperatures on the Barrier. This in turn could mean that the Polar party
would be unlikely to return to base camp before the ship had to return to
New Zealand in late February; so they would have to stay a further year.

On 28 October, three days before the main party set out, Scott wrote
from Winter Quarters to Mrs Lois Evans: [7]

> Dear Mrs Evans,
>
> Although I have never met you, your husband told me a great deal about you, so
> that I can imagine that you and the children will be wanting to see him home
> again next year, and will be very disappointed if he isn't able to come.
>
> So I write to tell you that he is very well indeed, very strong and in very
> good condition.
>
> It is possible we may not finish our work this year, and in that case he will
> stop with me for a second season.

If so you must try and remember that he is certain to be in the best of health, and that it will be all the better when he does come home.

When that time comes I hope he will get some good billet and not have to leave you again.

He is such an old friend of mine, and has done so well on this Expedition that he deserves all I can do for him.

So I must hope you won't be anxious or worried.

Yours sincerely,
R. Scott.

NOTES

1. Letter at SM.

2. *Hamlet*, Act III, scene 1.

3. Scott received £20 a week, Wilson and Lieutenant Evans £10, Bowers £4 4s., and the scientific staff £4; as a Chief Petty Officer, Edgar received 17s. 6d.

4. SPRI.

5. SM: 11 June 1962, letter to Mr Stanley Richards

6. ibid., 25 May 1962.

7. *SWDP*, 13 February 1913.

CHAPTER 6

The Southern Journey

Four men in the two motor sledges set out at the end of October with their substantial loads. On 1 November 1911 another ten men, each leading a pony, set out from the base camp, followed by two men, each with a dog team. Edgar led the way with 'Snatcher', but they soon found evidence that the four-man motor party ahead were having difficulties. Both vehicles had to be abandoned once the big ends broke, so their loads were re-packed and hauled by the four men to the place where they were to await the main party. But the extra physical work was to take its toll of Lieutenant Evans and Chief Stoker Lashly two months later, when the choice was made as to who would constitute the Polar party, and who would turn back as the Second Support Party.

In 1911 the motorised tractors were still in the experimental stage, and the Antarctic temperatures too low for them to function properly. But Scott's decision to use motorised transport would be vindicated with the use of Sno-Cats in Sir Vivian Fuchs's 1957–8 Commonwealth Trans-Antarctic Expedition.

Once the sixteen men met up—ten with the ponies, two with the dog teams, and four from the motor party—the loads were re-distributed. The other two members of the motor party—motor engineer Day (who had been with Shackleton in the *Nimrod*) and steward Hooper—turned back to base on 25 November, while the others proceeded across the Great Ice Barrier.

In early December they were held up unexpectedly for four days by a blizzard. This was a most frustrating delay with consumption of food and fuel, but no advance. The ponies, whose condition had delayed their start until the end of October, were unable to cope with the work and the conditions—indeed it was only through the care of Captain Oates that the ponies fulfilled their purpose of reaching the foot of the Beardmore Glacier. Here the remaining ones were shot, their meat partly fed to the dogs and partly depoted. Then the dog teams turned back to the base camp.

Now there were three teams of four men, each man-hauling a sledge for 134 miles up the Beardmore Glacier to reach the Polar plateau and an altitude of 10,000 feet. Edgar was with Captain Oates and Dr Wilson in the group led by Captain Scott, each man pulling nearly 200 pounds in weight. Unknown to them, Amundsen's party of five had used a different route to reach the Polar plateau, and attained the South Pole on 14 December.

A few days later Scott announced who would comprise the First Support Party, the four men to turn back in latitude 85 degrees 3 minutes south, at the top of the Beardmore Glacier. Lieutenant Atkinson would take back the Canadian Charles Wright, along with Cherry-Garrard and Petty Officer Keohane. All were naturally disappointed, especially Cherry-Garrard who had acquitted himself well during the winter journey. Wilson told him that he himself expected to go back on the next Support Party, as he presumed that Scott would take on three naval men to the Pole.

Figure 15. The western and depot parties. From the left: Griffith Taylor, Charles Wright, Lieut. Evans, Lieut. Bowers, Capt. Scott, Frank Debenham, Sub-Lieut. Gran, PO Edgar Evans, PO Thomas Crean. (Popperfoto)

Figure 16.   Edgar Evans bandaging Surgeon-Lieut. Atkinson's frostbitten hand, 5 July 1911.
(Popperfoto)

This left two parties of men to haul the sledges across the plateau. The South Pole was 340 miles away. Besides Scott's team, Lieutenant 'Teddy' Evans led the other one comprising Lieutenant Bowers and the two *Discovery* veterans, Crean and Lashly.

On Christmas Day, his forty-fourth birthday, Chief Stoker William Lashly fell down a crevasse. On being hauled up he was greeted with seasonal and birthday compliments: his reply was unrepeatable, but taken in good humour!

In his journal, Scott described Edgar Evans as

> A giant worker with a really remarkable head-piece. It is only now I realise how much has been due to him. Our ski shoes and crampons have been absolutely indispensable, and if the original ideas were not his, the details of manufacture, design and the good workmanship are his alone. He is responsible for every sledge, every sledge fitting, tents, sleeping bags, harness, and when one cannot recall a single expression of dissatisfaction with any of these items, it shows what an invaluable assistant he has been. Now, besides superintending the putting up of the tent, he thinks out and arranges the packing of the sledge; it is extraordinary how neatly and handily everything is stowed, and how much study has been given to preserving the suppleness and good running of the machine. On the Barrier, before the ponies were killed, he was ever roaming around, correcting faults of storage.

On 1 January 1912, Crean, Evans and Lashly were occupied in shortening the sledges from twelve feet to ten feet, in order to lighten them and to improve their running: eight hours' work in freezing conditions. Edgar cut his hand, but the severity of the injury was not evident at that time. However, the climate was uncongenial to healing, and the cut festered through lack of vitamin C.

Two days later Scott made his choice known. He would take his party on towards the Pole — Edgar Evans (aged 35), Dr Wilson (39), Captain Oates (31) and Scott himself (43). But he also added Lieutenant Bowers (28), making a party of five instead of four, with the Second Support Party comprising Lieutenant Evans with Crean and Lashly.

His choice drastically upset the logistics of the plans, which had been based around teams of four men, not five. The tents were designed for four people, the food was in units of four, the cookers took four servings (an extra twenty minutes was needed to heat up the fifth portion, as well as using more fuel), and they were accustomed to teams of four pulling each

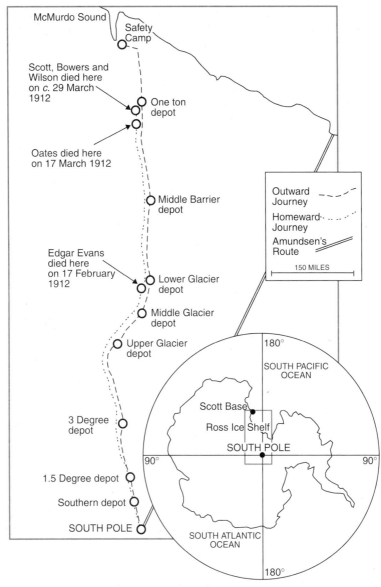

Figure 17. Map of the route to the Pole. (Viv Lewis)

sledge. Lieutenant Evans's party had been ordered to depot their skis earlier, so when Bowers joined the Polar party he had to proceed without skis for several weeks.

Lieutenant Evans, Crean and Lashly turned back at latitude 87 degrees 32 minutes south. Although greatly disappointed, the Second Support Party gave three cheers as they watched their five comrades march towards the Pole, 150 miles away: it was the last sight of them alive.

All five men were now feeling the effects of hard physical work on a insufficient diet. For 109 days their daily allowance per man had been:

16oz special biscuits, made by Huntley and Palmer
12oz pemmican (lean meat, dried and ground to a fine powder, mixed with lard and cast into blocks)
2oz butter
3oz sugar cubes
.57oz cocoa
.7oz tea

This was deficient in calories and vitamins, and totally lacking in vitamin C. It amounted to around 4,500 calories per man, which was between 1,000–1,500 calories too low for men labouring under such conditions as they were.[1] Knowledge of vitamins occurred too late to assist the British Antarctic Expedition.

After the satisfaction of passing Shackleton's 'furthest south', they found the conditions on the Polar plateau very hard. There was 50 degrees of frost at night, and deep sastrugi (snow waves caused by the wind) which made hauling the sledge particularly difficult. All five men were getting very tired, and the monotony of journeying through what Scott called 'a scene of wild desolation' was taking its toll.

Hitherto they would have assumed that the Beardmore Glacier was the route that the Norwegians would have used, and so finding no sign of them would have concluded that Amundsen had not reached the Polar plateau. But after one false start the Norwegians had found a different route, and took their dog teams up what they named the Axel-Heiberg Glacier, reaching the South Pole on 14 December.

For the British party it was on 16 January that their worst fears were realised: Lieutenant Bowers noticed a black spot in the distance, and on

Figure 18. Herbert Ponting's 1911 photograph of PO Edgar Evans.   (Popperfoto)

getting nearer they found it to be a black flag over a cairn, and they knew then that the Norwegians had forestalled them. Scott commented, 'It is a terrible disappointment, and I am very sorry for my loyal companions. All the day dreams must go; it will be a wearisome return'.

So it was a hollow triumph the following day when they made camp near the South Pole, and found a tent left by the Norwegians with a note from Amundsen. The temperature was minus 28 degrees Fahrenheit. Scott commented, 'Now we must face eight hundred miles of solid dragging. Great God! This is an awful place'. On the 18th they took photographs of themselves, and then prepared for the return journey, after already two and a half months of travel. Scott wrote in his journal, 'Now for the run home and a desperate struggle. I wonder if we can do it'.

Hopes of hoisting a sail on the sledge to assist them back across the plateau were blighted by wind that was either of insufficient strength or else from the wrong direction.

Edgar, Oates and Bowers were all suffering from frostbite, and Edgar also had an injured hand. The psychological impact of not having achieved priority at the Pole must have demoralised them. If they anticipated a return home to ridicule or apathy, how could they envisage the profound public feeling of admiration there would later be for their tragic endeavour?

Descending the Beardmore Glacier they got into a maze of crevasses, and on 4 February both Edgar and Scott separately had crevasse falls, with Edgar injuring his head. What might otherwise have been a small injury seems to have been far more serious, for he declined sharply after this. Up to then he was coping with an injured hand, frostbite, the acute disappointment of not being first at the Pole, and exhaustion from intense physical work in extremely cold conditions. It seems highly likely that the diet deficient in vitamin C meant that all five men were in the early stages of scurvy. This produces fragility in the blood vessels, so the head injury may have triggered off a brain haemorrhage which was to cause Edgar's death within two weeks: the fact that he kept going that long says much for his determination. Obviously the critical state of the party and the conditions would preclude any possibility of a post-mortem on him, so one cannot be dogmatic.

Wilson noted in his diary, 'Evans's collapse has much to do with the fact that he has never been sick in his life and is now helpless with his hands frostbitten'. Oates commented, 'He's quite worn out with the work, and how he's going to do the 400 odd miles we've still got to do I don't know'. Scott wrote that Edgar 'was a good deal run down. His fingers are badly blistered and his nose is rather seriously congested with frostbites'. His hands were 'really bad, and he shows signs of losing heart over it.'

By 14 February Edgar was no longer capable of camping work, and on the 16th near the Lower Glacier depot he collapsed with giddiness and vomiting. Scott noted, 'Evans has nearly broken down in brain, we think. He is absolutely changed from his normal self-reliant self'. The following day his journal recorded:

> *Saturday, February 17.* A very terrible day. Evans looked a little better after a good sleep and declared, as he always did, that he was quite well. He started in his place on the traces, but half an hour later worked his ski shoes adrift and had to leave the sledge. The surface was awful... We stopped after about one hour and Evans came up again but very slowly. Half an hour later he dropped out again on the same plea. He asked Bowers to lend him a piece of string. I cautioned him to come on as quickly as he could, and he answered cheerfully, as I thought. We had to push on, and the remainder of us were forced to pull very hard, sweating heavily. Abreast the Monument Rock we stopped, and seeing Evans a long way astern, I camped for lunch. There was no alarm at first, and we prepared tea and our own meal, consuming the latter. After lunch, and Evans still not appearing, we looked out to see him still afar off. By this time we were alarmed, and all four started back on ski.

> I was the first to reach the poor man and was shocked at his appearance; he was on his knees with clothing disarranged, hands uncovered and frost-bitten, and a wild look in his eyes. Asked what was the matter, he replied with a slow speech that he didn't know, but thought he must have fainted. We got him on his feet, but after two or three steps he sank down again. He showed every sign of complete collapse. Wilson, Bowers and I went back for the sledge, whilst Oates remained with him. When we returned he was practically unconscious, and when we got him into the tent, quite comatose. He died quietly at 12.30 am. On discussing the symptoms, we think he began to get weaker just before we reached the Pole, and that his downward path was accelerated, first by the shock of his frost-bitten fingers, and later by falls during rough travelling on the glacier, further by his loss of all confidence in himself. Wilson thinks it certain he must have injured his brain by a fall.

The first intimation that all might not be well with the Polar Party was received a few days later. Petty Officer Crean reached the old *Discovery* hut after marching alone for eighteen hours, covering thirty-five miles. He brought the news that Lieutenant Evans had collapsed with scurvy, and was being nursed on the Barrier by Stoker Lashly. Fortunately Surgeon

Atkinson was at the hut with the Russian dog handler Dimitri and the dog teams, and after a blizzard had passed they were able to rescue the two men. Atkinson remained with Lieutenant Evans at Hut Point, and a message was sent to Cape Evans to bring up the *Terra Nova* from the base camp, where she had been unloading fresh stores since arriving from New Zealand a month before.

When the vessel reached Hut Point 'Teddy' Evans was conveyed in his sleeping bag on board, and placed in the Captain's cabin. There Sub-Lieutenant Gran, the young Norwegian on the expedition as a skiing instructor, spoke privately with him on 29 February. From this conversation Gran concluded that the prospects for the five-man Polar party were not so bright as had been imagined, since Lieutenant Evans's frightful journey indicated what Scott and his companions might expect, with the Polar winter drawing in. The *Terra Nova* sailed back to New Zealand, taking those persons not staying for a further winter, and 'Teddy' Evans was invalided home to Britain.

As the main group was at Cape Evans, two men remained at Hut Point with an arrangment of signal lights to relay the first news of the return of the Polar party. Gran's diary (written in Norwegian) reveals the increasing anxiety about the fate of the five men. [2]

> *6 March:* 'The polar party should not be far from its goal now [meaning Hut Point], if all goes well.'
>
> *7 March:* 'The polar party can now be expected any day.'
>
> *13 March:* 'The polar party should be back now.'
>
> *14 March:* 'If Scott maintains the same average speed as Shackleton, he must be back now.'

Of course, Scott and the others were maintaining no such speed — from sixteen or seventeen miles a day they were managing only four or five by this time.

Captain Oates was the next to succumb. Scurvy can cause the re-opening of wounds which have healed years before, and Oates had received a thigh wound in 1901, during an heroic action in Cape Province at the time of the South African war. Some felt that he should have been awarded the Victoria

Cross for his conduct on that occasion, but now 'Never-say-die' Oates was being called upon to show his mettle in a cause that was already lost.

For weeks he would have been trudging along in agony, and Wilson admitted that there was nothing they could do for him. On 16 March Oates lay down in his sleeping bag hoping that he would not awake the next morning. But he did, and uttering the famous words, 'I am just going outside and I may be some time', he crawled out of the tent to his death in a blizzard. It was his thirty-second birthday, and a month since Edgar's death. Scott wrote in his journal: 'We knew it was the act of a brave man and an English gentleman', and he added that they resolved to meet their end, when it came, 'with a similar spirit'.

Back at Cape Evans, awaiting the signal from Hut Point that the Polar party had arrived, Gran wrote on 20 March:

> I thought the hut would fly apart in the night, so strong was the wind. It can't be easy to travel on the Barrier in such God forsaken weather. Let's hope our people have reached Hut Point.

Figure 19. At the South Pole, 18 January 1912. Standing: Capt. L.E.G. Oates, Capt. R.F. Scott, PO Edgar Evans; seated: Lieut. H.R. Bowers, Dr E.A. Wilson. Bowers holds the string to release the camera shutter. Wilson's eyes are bandaged because of snow blindness.   (Popperfoto)

23 March: 'If the Polar party are not back yet there must be grounds for anxiety. It looks like foul weather again.'

25 March: 'We have begun to worry a little about the fate of the polar party. No one says anything, but you can see it in most of their faces. When the watchman comes down from Vane Hill each night to report, everything comes to a standstill in the hut, and every eye is fixed on him.'

Scott, Bowers and Wilson pitched camp twice more after Oates's death, but were overtaken by a ten-day blizzard when eleven miles short of One Ton Depot. Writing the letter which he addressed 'to my widow', Scott said:

What lots and lots I could tell you of this journey. How much better it has been than lounging about in too great comfort at home. What tales you would have had for the boy [the future Sir Peter Scott], but oh, what a price to pay.

He also wrote to his friend, the playright Sir J.M. Barrie [creator of 'Peter Pan'], asking him to ensure that his widow and the widow of Edgar Evans were provided for. That says much of Scott's feeling of responsibility for his men, and his regard for Edgar.

Scott's final journal entry was dated Thursday, 29 March 1912, stating that outside the door of the tent was still a scene of whirling drift, that they were getting weaker, and that the end could not be far off. His postscript 'For God's sake look after our people' reveals his anxiety about the official verdict on an expedition which had not achieved priority at the South Pole, and which left behind substantial debts and five families bereaved. Scott was not to know the impact that the news of those five deaths would make, nor could he conceive that the tragedy would be elevated to one of the most heroic of British exploits.

NOTES

1. A.F. Rogers, 'The Death of Chief Petty Officer Edgar Evans', *The Practitioner* (April 1974), pp. 570–80

2. The excerpts from the diaries are taken from *The Norwegian with Scott* (HMSO, London), for which I am indebted to the editor, Dr Geoffrey Hattersley-Smith, and the translator, Mrs Ellen-Johanne McGhie, daughter of Major Tryggve Gran.

CHAPTER 7

The Relief Expedition

On 1 April 1912 the *Terra Nova* reached New Zealand, to hear of Amundsen's success at the Pole, and to tell who comprised the Polar party of the British expedition. With Lieutenant 'Teddy' Evans on board with scurvy, the vessel's commander, Lieutenant Pennell, was concerned to allay any fears Mrs Lois Evans might have had that her own husband's condition could be similarly precarious. As we know, she would have had good cause to be anxious, for unbeknown to them all Edgar had died six weeks earlier. Lieutenant Pennell wrote to her: [1]

Dear Mrs Evans,

I am writing to you to supplement the telegram sent home by Captain Scott, as I am afraid you may be anxious at not hearing from your husband.

The sole reason is the one mentioned in the telegram, namely that Capt. Scott started late as a matter of policy, and so was late returning, and the season closed particularly early, so that the ship had to leave earlier than hoped.

In respect to Lieut. Evans contracting scurvy — I should like to point out that this case was very exceptional — as he was the only one of the main party out sledging just before they started, and so was on sledging rations while all the others (including your husband) were on fresh food in the hut.

In fact there need be no anxiety as regards the others in respect to scurvy. The last reports of your husband are that he was in the very best of health and spirits, and I heartily congratulate you on his being in the Polar Party, for there can be little doubt that they will reach the Pole, though of course the news cannot come through for a year.

I am
Yours sincerely
Harry Pennell.

At Cape Evans, Gran noted in his diary:

> *5 April:* 'Calm again tonight with moonshine and 25 degrees centigrade of frost,
> so I shouldn't be surprised if Scott were to arrive on Easter Sunday.'

But five days later he wrote, 'Alas, our fears of last month are justified. The polar party have still not returned to Hut Point: their fate must be sealed.'

The following day, 11 April, Gran noted, 'Scott and his team must have met their deaths, given that they're still on the Barrier—that we are all agreed upon. Scott's goal was the South Pole... it is our duty to find him and see whether documentary proof can also be found.'

While those at Cape Evans knew that the five men must have perished, but were ignorant of whether they had reached the Pole, the outside world knew that Amundsen had been first at that desolate spot. But the attention of the English speaking world was arrested by a major maritime disaster that would seem to dwarf concern over a mere five men in Antarctica: on 15 April the SS *Titanic* sank in the north Atlantic on her maiden voyage, with the loss of 1,513 lives.

In the hut at Cape Evans, Tryggve Gran continued expressing their feelings in his diary:

> *18 April:* 'Cherry-Garrard has told us of fearful, indescribable days and nights
> out on the Barrier. As soon as the sun went down the temperature would at once
> sink to -50 degrees C . How on earth could the Polar party hope to suceed in
> such conditions, sick and worn out as they must have been after a journey of
> 2,600 km? Poor Dr Wilson, you deserved a better fate.'

Cherry-Garrard was by then the only man living who had experienced a wintertime Antarctic journey.

Yet hope must have flickered for a few more days, until, on 1 May, Gran wrote: 'The five who are out on the Barrier can, alas, no longer be counted among the living'. Two days later he noted that he had performed the sad duty of tidying up Wilson and Scott's cubicles.

During that Antarctic winter of 1912 Lieutenant Atkinson, the sole British officer present, encouraged every member of the depleted group to share in discussing future plans. There was the predicament of Campbell's Northern Party, but the possibility that the *Terra Nova* might have been able to collect them when she steamed north in March to New Zealand. Equally those six men might be able to make their own way to the hut after the winter (this was what in fact they did). If a relief expedition went south for remains of the Polar party it might find no trace — Atkinson for one felt they might have all fallen into a crevasse. Yet all agreed that for the sake of the next of kin, and to complete the records of the expedition, an attempt should be made to find whether Scott had achieved his objective of reaching the South Pole, and what was their fate.

Back in England, Kathleen Scott had received her husband's diary, and wrote on 19 August from Sandwich, Kent, to Lois Evans. [2] Both women were unaware then that they had been widowed.

> I think you will be glad to hear how well he [Captain Scott] speaks throughout it of your husband and his work. Apparently he has made himself more than useful, he has worked so hard and so willingly through every sort of difficulty — and finally has been chosen to go on to the Pole. I am sure you will like to hear how indispensable he has made himself to Captain Scott and how fit and hardworking and thorough he has been — my husband asked me to tell you how splendid he has been....

But life in Portsmouth was becoming difficult for Lois Evans with her three young children. After two years the funds of the expedition were exhausted, for the seamen were off the Naval payroll throughout this time. For the remainder of 1912 the family were in increasingly straightened circumstances. [3]

On 29 October 1912, a year after the Southern Journey had commenced, the Relief Expedition set out. Canadian Charles Wright led the way as navigator, leading the men with six Indian mules, brought down by the *Terra Nova* for the second season. This group comprised Crean and Lashly from the Second Support Party, Hooper from the Motor Party, the biologist Nelson, Sub-Lieutenant Gran, and Petty Officers Keohane and Williamson. Thomas Williamson was a *Discovery* veteran who had been transferred to the shore party when the *Terra Nova* sailed from Cape Evans in March 1912, taking back those who were not staying for a second year. Behind them came the Russian dog handler Dimitri with the two dog teams, and Lieutenant Atkinson and Cherry-Garrard, both from the First Support Party. Debenham and Archer remained behind at the hut.

They reached One Ton Depot on 11 November, and found no sign that the Polar party had been there. That must have been some solace to Cherry-Garrard, who with Dimitri and the dog teams had waited several days at the depot in early March: during the winter he must have agonised over whether he had turned back too soon.

The following day, 12 November 1912, the men saw Wright veer over towards the right. He had noticed what appeared to be a cairn. Some snow was kicked away, and the tent's air-vent was revealed. They waited until Atkinson came up, and then cleared away more snow. Atkinson took inside the oldest man in the party, Chief Stoker William Lashly, the man who along with Crean and Lieutenant Evans had been the last to see the Polar party alive. Lashly emerged with tears in his eyes.

Atkinson took the men one at a time into the tent to see the bodies of Scott, with Bowers and Wilson on either side of him. Then Atkinson went into his tent to read Scott's journal, diligently written in pencil under the most exacting conditions, and afterwards he assembled the men and told them what had happened. Crean congratulated Gran on the success of his fellow-countrymen, though both men were too moved to say more.

Gran noted in his diary:

> On the return journey, during the descent of the Beardmore Glacier, Petty Officer Evans fell down a crevasse and was injured. Right from the Pole itself they had noticed a great change in this big, strong man, and the fall seemed to take toll of the rest of his vitality. The fact that Amundsen was first at the Pole in a way meant more to Evans than the rest. Had Scott been first, Evans would have achieved financial independence, but now the future must have seemed uncertain and unattractive.

The Relief Expedition moved on to look for the body of Captain Oates. They recovered his sleeping bag where it had been discarded, but his body had been buried by the winter snowfalls. Near the place of his death they erected a memorial, 'Hereabouts died a very gallant gentleman'. Returning to the last camp of Scott, Bowers and Wilson, they collapsed the tent rods and built a large cairn over their grave.

When they returned to the Base Camp they were heartened to find that Campbell's Northern Party was safe, having made their way back after enduring immense privations throughout the winter. Atkinson handed over command to Lieutenant Campbell, and they prepared for the return of the *Terra Nova* from New Zealand to take them home.

   The deaths of the five men were not the only tragedies on the British
Antarctic Expedition, for on 17 August 1912 a member of the crew of the
Terra Nova, Chief Stoker Robert Brissenden, had drowned in New Zealand
waters.

   The vessel had left Port Lyttleton on 14 December, but took eighteen
days to break through the pack ice. Under Commander 'Teddy' Evans, now
recovered from scurvy and promoted while in England,[4] the *Terra Nova*
reached Cape Evans on 18 January. The ship had been cleaned and a
celebratory meal prepared for the five who had reached the Pole, although
those on board knew that Amundsen had achieved priority there. Packages
of letters from home were laid out for each person, with various luxuries
such as chocolates, champagne and cigars put ready for the men who had
spent two years in Antarctica.

   Seeing the excited figures on shore, Commander Evans called out
through a megaphone from the bridge, 'Are you all well?' His enquiry was
followed by an ominous pause, before Lieutenant Campbell replied, 'The
Southern Party reached the South Pole on 17th January last year, but were
all lost on the return journey — we have their records'. Eventually the order
to drop anchor broke the silence. Flags were lowered to half mast, and the
steward discreetly removed the packages and table settings. Each person's
mail had been placed in pillow-slips, on which the recipient's name was
boldly printed: now the undelivered letters were sealed up, for return to
wives and mothers.

   The ship's carpenter, Frank Davies, set to work making a nine foot cross
out of Australian jarrah wood. The personnel of the Relief Expedition
carried it by sledge to Hut Point, where it was erected on Observation Hill.
It stated the names of the five who had perished, and the final line of
Tennyson's poem *Ulysses* –

   To strive, to seek, to find, and not to yield.

   That site for the memorial cross, overlooking their old hut, would have
been familiar to Edgar and the two other veterans from the *Discovery*
expedition, Scott and Wilson.

   Then the *Terra Nova* sailed to New Zealand.

Besides the importance of informing next of kin of the tragedy, press contracts required that the vessel remain at sea for twenty-four hours after the news had been cabled to Britain. So amid some secrecy Lieutenants Atkinson and Pennell were rowed into the little harbour of Oamaru at night, while the ship sailed up and down the coast, ignoring the lighthouse's requests for identification. When he re-embarked, Atkinson remarked to Cherry-Garrard that the news had made a tremendous impression.

Early on Wednesday, 12 February 1913, white ensign flying at half mast, the *Terra Nova* entered Lyttleton harbour. Everywhere flags were at half mast—as Cherry-Garrard said, 'We landed to find the Empire— almost the civilised world—in mourning'.

NOTES

1. SM: Edgar Evans file.

2. ibid.

3. *SWEP*, 12 January 1994.

4. 'Teddy' Evans was later known as 'Evans of the Broke', following heroic action commanding the destroyer, HMS *Broke* in 1917. He became a Rear Admiral, and was elevated to the peerage in 1946 as Lord Mountevans. He died in 1957.

CHAPTER 8

Lois

Lois Evans and her children, Norman, Muriel and Ralph, had moved back to Gower in January 1913. Mr William Tucker, a relative from Pitton Cross Farm, [1] travelled down to Portsmouth and brought them back with him. They were staying with Lois's parents, who had by then relinquished the 'Ship Inn' and moved to West Pilton Cottage. During the afternoon of 10 February Lois was looking for cockles on the beach at Oxwich with her youngest child Ralph and fourteen year old Lilly Tucker. [2] Her father had taken them there in his pony and trap, but after only a few hours Lilly was surprised to see him coming across the sand towards them. He was carrying a telegram from New Zealand, forwarded from Portsmouth. It said, 'Members wish to express deepest sympathy in your sad loss. Commander Evans.'

Although the news of the tragedy was in the Swansea papers that Monday evening, and Norman and Muriel heard something of it at school, the meaning of the telegram only became clear the following morning. A reporter from the *South Wales Daily Post* called at West Pilton Cottage with details of what had been reported, and there was a telegram from Lois's brother Stanley, in the Navy in Devonport: 'Just read terrible news; try to bear up: will write — Stan'. [3]

Lois, described patronisingly as 'quite a superior and refined little woman', [4] told the press, 'I have this consolation — he died bravely'. She said,

> I received a bundle of letters last May which had been brought to New Zealand by Commander Evans when he left the party. These were about fifty in number and covered the period of a whole year. The last one which though undated appeared either to have been written in December 1911 or January of last year, was written in pencil. It stated that he was only 150 miles from the Pole. [5]

Edgar's mother, then a seventy year old widow, was living nearby with her sister Mrs Powell, in Pitton. She said, 'I was always proud of my boy and I am prouder than ever to know that he died a hero's death'. [6]

The obituary in the *South Wales Daily News* [7] stated:

His Career

> Born in Gower, Seaman Evans came with his family when quite young to Swansea, and was educated at the National Schools. On leaving school he was for a time in service at the Swansea Castle Hotel. Becoming fascinated with the sea, at the age of 16 he entered the Navy, and at the time of his death had three years to serve before becoming entitled to a pension. It was while in the Navy that he attracted the notice of Captain Scott, whom he joined on his first Antarctic expedition about 10 years ago. Invited to join the second expedition, he promptly accepted. In the interval between the two expeditions he married Lois Bevan [*sic*] daughter of Mr and Mrs William Bevan, who then kept the Old Ship Inn at Middleton. It was from the cliffs near here that he saw the *Terra Nova* enter the Bristol Channel en route for Cardiff just before she started on what was for him his last cruise — a cruise which, while having so sad an ending, has left his name enrolled in history as one of the first band of brave Britishers to stand where till a few weeks previously no human foot had stood before — an example of what intrepid manhood and determination can perform over almost insuperable obstacles. And now his body lies embalmed in ice in an honoured grave nearer the South Pole than any other in existence.

The memorial service for all five men was held at St Paul's Cathedral on Friday, 14 February, with King George V leading the mourners. It was estimated that as many as ten thousand persons stood outside.

On the evening of Sunday, 16 February in Gower there was a memorial service at St Mary's church, Rhosili. The *Gower Church Magazine* reported:

> Naval Petty Officer Edgar Evans, in charge of the sledges and equipment, of whom Capt. Scott's last message pathetically speaks as the 'strong man of the party, — the man whom we had least expected to fail', belonged to Rhosili, about twenty miles west of Swansea. He and his wife, who is living with her mother and father and her three children at Rhosili, were first cousins. They were married at Rhosili Church eight years ago. Evans joined the Navy at the age of sixteen. He had risen to a gunnery instructorship and would shortly have been entitled to his pension. His first Polar expedition was in 1901, when he went with Capt. Scott in the *Discovery*. A thrill of sympathy was felt all over the world on receiving the tragic news of the death of the five heroes on their return journey after the discovery of the South Pole. Rich and poor have sent messages

of heartfelt sympathy with those who have been stricken with grief and have suffered such a loss.

Elsewhere in Gower there were memorial services for Edgar at the churches in Pennard and Ilston, and in Swansea at Holy Trinity, at St Mary's, St Paul's Sketty, St Mark's Waun Wen, Mount Pleasant Baptist, the Wesley Chapel, and Capel Gomer, while at Swansea's Albert Hall prayers were offered for the bereaved in Gower.[8]

Lois received a letter from Commander 'Teddy' Evans, dated 5 February,[9] written on board the *Terra Nova* before she reached New Zealand:

Dear Mrs Evans,

I am writing to sympathise with you on your terrible bereavement.

Your husband died a gallant death on the return march from the Pole after faithfully serving his leader, Capt. Scott, through a most trying time.

He lost his life for the honour of his country, and the British Navy will be proud of having possessed such a brave man. His 'grit' will for ever be an example to the lower deck, his ability was remarkable and I wish to convey to you from the whole Expedition our sorrow.

I also write to tell you of the admiration we felt for your dead husband.

I shall soon be in England, and I will see that you and yours never want. If you are in immediate need write at once to:

Mr Wilkinson Greene,
Secretary to Sir Edgar Speyer Bart,
7 Lothbury, London E.C.

I cannot tell you how sorry I am for you.
Believe me,
Your sincere friend

Edward G.R. Evans
Commander R.N.

Amongst the other letters of condolence was one from Lieutenant Atkinson,[10] dated 31 January, who wrote:

I have a very sad duty to perform in writing to you the news of your husband's death on his return from the South Pole in February 1912. He had a very severe fall coming down the Beardmore Glacier and hurt his head. Captain Scott and his companions stuck by him, but he got much worse and died on the 7th [sic] February and was buried there, at the foot of the Glacier by them. Your husband on many occasions has shown me very great kindness, and in any way I can repay it, it would give me great pleasure… his diary from the South Pole will be sent to you…

Other tributes [11] included one dated 11 February 1913 which stated that 'The Royal Humane Society records its deepest sympathy and condolence to the relatives of Seaman (Petty Officer) Edgar Evans R.N.'. Moreover, on 19 February 1913, the British Schools and University Club of New York sent Lois a three page calligraphic presentation address. Perhaps in Edgar's case it was not strictly accurate to say, 'overcome in that Polar desert, they died for the honour of *England*…' After the Memorial Service at St Paul's the parents of Commander Evans wrote to Lois: 'It is only the Will of Providence that one Evans was taken instead of another'.

Lois returned briefly to Portsmouth before moving to Morriston, the suburb in northern Swansea that was the centre of the tinplate industry. Her elder sister, Beatrice, was married to iron merchant John Faull, and they lived at Falmouth House in Clydach Road, Morriston. There, on 4 May, Lois received a visit from Commander Evans, who had travelled by a P. and O. liner from New Zealand ahead of the *Terra Nova*, and motored down from Cardiff with his friend, Percy Lewis. [12]

'Teddy' Evans was himself recently bereaved, for his New Zealand-born wife, Hilda, had died on board ship of peritonitis while accompanying her husband back to Britain. Commander Evans said that he wished to call on Lois to deliver her husband's pocket-book to her. It was sealed with two government seals, so that it should only be opened by her, and Commander Evans said he felt it appropriate that it should be handed over by one of those who last saw her husband alive. As with all other members' diaries, Lois was not permitted to publish any of it for two years.

Their meeting was private, with just Ralph (aged four and a half) present. Afterwards Lois said she was pleased with the arrangements made by the government and the Mansion House committee for her future: she would receive a lump sum of £1,250 from the Memorial Fund, as well as a pension of £48 a year, as the Admiralty had decided that they would regard the loss of the Naval men as if they had been killed in action. Commander Evans described Lois as 'the brave widow of a brave man'.

The financial arrangements precluded taking up the 'generous offer' [13] of the London Orphanage Asylum, whose Board of Managers had offered to admit free of charge one of Edgar's children, in recognition of the bravery and heroism of their father. The child would have been maintained and educated until the age of fifteen.

In July, survivors of the expedition attended an investiture at Buckingham Palace, where P.O. Thomas Crean and Chief Stoker William Lashly received the Albert Medal for saving the life of Commander Evans, and Herbert Ponting's film of the Expedition was shown. Polar medals were awarded, with Lois receiving the one for her husband.

The weekly Swansea paper, The *Cambrian*, had called for '... at Swansea or in Gower some permanent memorial to the honour of Petty Officer Evans, who thus links this locality with one of the most heroic exploits of the British race'. [14] Similarly the mayor of Swansea said, 'This is an occasion when the whole country will take the matter up. But there is also the local aspect, and in movements of this kind Swansea has never been behind'. [15] As it turned out quite the reverse was the case, for the only local memorial in the short term was the plaque inside Rhosili church, erected on Tuesday, 27 January 1914.

The *Gower Church Magazine* [16] reported:

> A beautiful memorial tablet has been erected in Rhosili Church to the memory of the late Mr Edgar Evans, Chief Petty Officer, who accompanied Captain Scott to the utmost point of the South Pole, and who perished on the return journey, to be much lamented by his widow and widowed mother, both at the time the news reached this country residing in Rhosili Parish.

The Tablet is inscribed as follows:

To the Glory of God

in the memory of

EDGAR EVANS

> 1st Class Petty Officer, R.N., and a native of this Parish, who perished on the 17th Feb. 1912 when returning from the South Pole with the Southern Party of the British Antarctic Expedition under the command of Captain Robert Falcon Scott, C.V.O., R.N.

'To seek, to strive, to find, and not to yield.'

Erected by Lois Evans

    The Sunday following the rector preached the following sermon which many would be glad to read as it refers to the conduct and lives of the five brave men who did so much to honour our race and country. I may add that it gives me much pleasure to record the substantial sympathy shown by the Government and the general public for those who were dependent upon the fallen heroes and that therefore no anxiety need be felt as to future provision for their comfort and happiness.

The rector (who had performed the wedding ceremony of Edgar and Lois nearly ten years earlier) said:

One whose memorial tablet has been erected in this his native parish will go down to posterity as one who was deemed worthy to be chosen among the few last selected out of a band of heroes to accompany Capt. Scott to the South Pole. The words spoken of him by the Captain ring in our ears today. He was the strong man of the party — one with a wonderful head, equal to any emergency, and brave to face any difficulty — one who on the return journey was the first to perish through exhaustion and disease. There he lies amid the eternal ice, a monument of courage and resource at the farthest point from living humanity,

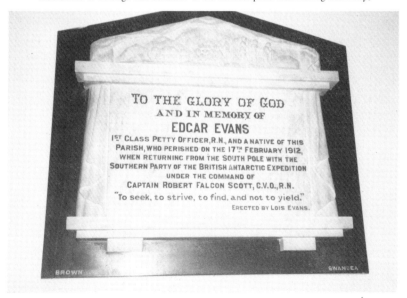

Figure 20. Plaque inside Rhosili church.   (Jane Gregor)

but never to be forgotten by his country nor to fade from its annals. These men, having accomplished their heroic task, were unable to return to tell the tale to their proud countrymen, but they left behind them records which have been faithfully treasured and which will prove to be of great value in the further pursuit of scientific research. All honour to them for their arduous task completed, and the way they met death redounds to the glory of our race. They were loyal and true to each other to the last. As comrades they showed the greatest care and kindness to each other, and taught afresh to a world growing more luxurious and effeminate, the glory of a soldier's endurance and capacity for stern duty and the possession of scientific courage to the last.

On 13 February 1914 the *Cambrian* stated that, 'An additional grant from the Treasury has now placed the mother of Edgar Evans, the South Pole hero, beyond the necessity of receiving an old age pension'.

After the *Terra Nova* had returned to Cardiff on 13 June 1913 — almost three years to the day since she had left — the ship was bought back by Bowring Brothers of Liverpool and Newfoundland. F.C. Bowring presented to the city a clock tower in the shape of a lighthouse, which was sited in Roath Park lake. The names of the Polar Party are on a plaque above the door.

Soon afterwards, the country was plunged into the Great War, and although various memorials to Scott were erected, the impetus for any further memorial to Edgar Evans subsided. Lois and her children settled in Cwmrhydyceirw, the suburb adjoining Morriston, naming their house in Llys Fedw 'Terra Nova'.

On 30 December 1948, Lois was among those who attended the premiere of the Royal Command film, *Scott of the Antarctic*, at the Odeon, Leicester Square. John Mills played the part of Scott, while James Robertson Justice took the part of Edgar, though without attempting any Welsh accent.

Lois died at the age of seventy-three on 23 April 1952 in Gorseinon Hospital, near where her daughter Muriel lived since her marriage. The *South Wales Evening Post* [17] reported:

Widow of Swansea Antarctic hero dead.

The death was announced yesterday from Gorseinon hospital of Mrs Lois Evans, widow of Petty Officer (Taff) Evans. Mrs Evans, who was aged 73, was a native of Swansea, and lived at 'Terra Nova', Heol-y-Fedw, Cwmrhydyceirw,

Morriston. Petty Officer Edgar Evans died with the Captain Scott Expedition to the Antarctic. Mrs Evans, with her two sons, attended a special showing of the film 'Scott of the Antarctic' which was shown in London on December 30th 1948. While in London she met the sisters of Captain Scott and Captain Oates, and the sister of Dr Wilson.

Mrs Evans was a member of St David's Church, Morriston. She leaves two sons Norman and Ralph, and one daughter, Muriel.

Sadly, during her lifetime it would have seemed that the only initiative to honour her husband was that taken by herself: at least the fruition of later efforts has occurred during the time of two of her children.

NOTES

1. *WM*, 12 February 1913.

2. *SWEP*, 12 January 1994.

3. *SWDP*, 11 February 1913.

4. *WM*, 12 February 1913.

5. *SWDP*, 11 February 1913.

6. ibid., 12 February 1913.

7. *South Wales Daily News*, 12 February 1913.

8. *SWDP*, 17 February 1913.

9. ibid., 13 February 1913.

10. SPRI: Sotheby's catalogue, 7 December 1984.

11. ibid.

12. *WM*, 5 May 1913.

13. ibid., 21 February 1913.

14. *Cambrian*, 14 February 1913.

15. *SWDP*, 14 February 1913.

16. *Gower Church Magazine*, March 1914.

17. *SWEP*, 24 April 1952. At her own request she is buried in an unmarked grave in Morriston cemetery, plot no 272A.

CHAPTER 9

Recognition

The post-war initiative to honour Edgar began through his niece, Mrs Sarah Owen, who as a young woman had gone on board the *Terra Nova* at Cardiff in 1910. Her reminiscences in 1954 provided the basis for an article, 'Edgar Evans. A Gower Hero' by Dr Gwent Jones, in volume vii of *Gower*, the annual journal of the Gower Society. Eight years later, her memories were likewise tapped for an article by Mr George Long of the *South Wales Evening Post,* [1] near the fiftieth anniversary of the Expedition's reaching the Pole. That article provoked the curator of Swansea Museum, Mr Stanley Richards, to campaign for a local memorial to Edgar Evans in the town centre, rebuilt following the devastation from the 'Three Nights' Blitz' in February 1941. Letters flowed to the local newspaper, and Mr Richards penned articles for various periodicals and papers.

Edgar's name was preserved in the continent where he died, by three New Zealand expeditions which named geographical features in New Zealand's Ross Dependency after him. [2] These are the Evans Piedmont Glacier (76 degrees 44'S, 162 degrees 40E) in Victoria Land, the Evans Glacier (83 degrees 47'S, 170 degrees 00'E), which flows east from the Queen Alexandra Range into the Beardmore Glacier, and the Evans Névé (72 degrees 45'S, 164 degrees 30'E).

Major recognition in Britain came initially from outside Wales. In 1964, HMS *Excellent*, The Royal Naval Gunnery School at Whale Island in Portsmouth, decided to name a new accommodation block 'The Edgar Evans Building'. Contact was made with Mr Richards, and, through him, invitations extended to members of the family to attend the opening on 18 December 1964. On that occasion, Sir Royston Wright, the Second Sea Lord, spoke of Edgar's 'strength of character, devotion, loyalty, and bravery'. [3]

Figure 21. 'Antarctic heroes' postcard. (John Davies)

Mr Richards had declined the invitation to attend, as he was being interviewed about Edgar that day at the Bristol studios of TWW (Television Wales and the West, the predecessor of HTV). He took along a plaster model of Edgar pulling a sledge, entitled 'A Giant Worker', which had been made and presented to Swansea Museum by former miner, George Evans (no relation) from Banwen, Neath. [4]

A newspaper suggestion that the story of Edgar should inspire a local artist was taken up by Mr John J. Jones of Morriston, a member of the Swansea Arts Society. He produced two oil paintings [5] in memory of Edgar, and presented them to the Museum.

The Head Post Office in Wind Street [6] displayed a framed photograph taken by Swansea photographer Henry Chapman at the time of Edgar's wedding in 1904. It is inscribed:

> Chief Petty Officer Edgar Evans RN (Ex-Boy Messenger at Swansea) who perished near the South Pole on the 17th February 1912 while a member of Captain Robert Falcon Scott's Antarctic Expedition.

Figure 22.   Philip Chatfield's bust of Edgar Evans.   (SWEP)

There appeared in the April 1974 issue of *The Practitioner* an article by Dr A.F. Rogers of the University of Bristol, entitled 'The Death of Chief Petty Officer Edgar Evans'. It analysed the rations for the sledging journeys, and concluded that they were inadequate for the hard physical work undertaken, and crucially deficient in vitamin C, thereby rendering the men liable to scurvy. In the early stages scurvy produces fragility in the blood vessels, so Dr Rogers concluded that Edgar's head injury from the crevasse fall on 4 February 1912 could have induced a brain haemorrhage that brought on his collapse and death thirteen days later. Dr Rogers is no armchair academic propounding his theories from an ivory tower: an expert on polar physiology, he accompanied Sir Vivian Fuchs on the 1957–8 Commonwealth Trans-Antarctic Expedition.

St Mary's Church in Swansea was presented in 1978 with an oak chair made by retired school carpenter and joiner, Mr Gwyn Morris. It is inscribed:

In memory of C.P.O. Edgar Evans

One of Captain Scott's ill-fated party of five to lose their lives after reaching the South Pole on January 17 1912. He fell on Beardmore Glacier on February 4 1912, and died on February 17 1912, at Lower Glacier Depot.

In November and December 1984 various letters and items of Edgar's, including his Polar medal, were sold at Sotheby's on behalf of members of the family.[7] Fortunately, his Navigating Officer's Notebook of the First Geological Journey 1911 was purchased by the Scott Polar Research Institute, Cambridge University.

Swansea City Council took over the running of Swansea Museum in late 1991, and in the course of much refurbishment, an exhibition about Edgar was displayed throughout 1993, with an accompanying booklet published. Further articles on Edgar appeared in *Gower*, the journal of the Gower Society, volumes xliv and xlv.

On the eighty-second anniversary of his death, a Civic Ceremony was held at the Brangwyn Hall, Swansea, on 17 February 1994, when Herbert Ponting's archive film of the Expedition, *90 Degrees South*, was shown. A bust of Edgar, taken from the famous photograph of him at the South Pole, was presented to the City of Swansea by the Lord Lieutenant of West Glamorgan, Sir Michael Llewellyn, who described Edgar as 'a very courageous man'. The Lord Mayor of Cardiff expressed the hope that the bust 'will have an honoured place in the city', and the Lord Mayor of Swansea said that Edgar 'had his roots firmly in south-west Gower', and conceded that 'perhaps his recognition has been much too long in coming'. Guest of honour at the ceremony was Edgar's eighty-seven year old daughter, Mrs Muriel Hawkins, with other members of the family present. Commissioned by the Captain Scott Society of Cardiff,[8] the port from which the *Terra Nova* had sailed, the bust was made in Gower of white Italian marble by sculptor Philip Chatfield, and later that year it was prominently sited in Swansea Museum.

Pupils from Edgar's old school, St Helen's, took part in the Civic Ceremony, and the school has an exhibition and display of children's work about their famous 'old boy';[9] they have links with HMS *Excellent* and have been presented with the ship's badge.[10]

As to why it took so long for Edgar to be officially recognised in his home area, one could suggest three main reasons. First, his rank as a seaman. The other four who perished returning from the Pole were all of officer or similar status. Lawrence Oates, who crawled out of the tent to his death a month after Edgar died, was a Captain in the 6th Royal Inniskilling Dragoons. Of the three who perished during a blizzard a fortnight later, Henry Bowers was a Lieutenant in the Royal Indian Marine, Dr Edward Wilson, a zoologist and chief of scientific staff on the British Antarctic Expedition, and Robert Falcon Scott, a Royal Naval Captain and leader of the Expedition.

By contrast, Edgar, in the phraseology of certain sections of the contemporary press, was 'merely' a seaman, the only member of the lower deck in the team: in fact he was a Chief Petty Officer, very much an integral member of the Expedition. Photographer Herbert Ponting had described him as 'one of the leader's towers of strength.... Nobody ever doubted, all through the winter, that Petty Officer Evans would be one of the ones chosen for the Pole. The party selected by Captain Scott were the four men who possessed the most striking personalities'. Writing a month before they reached the Pole, Scott described Edgar as 'A giant worker with a really remarkable headpiece. It is only now I realise how much has been due to him'.

Secondly, there was his alleged neglect of his family. During the *Discovery* expedition, Edgar had been a single man. By the time the *Terra Nova* sailed from Cardiff in June 1910 he was married with three young children. The Admiralty had granted leave for him and others to join this

Expedition, but they were off the Naval payroll during that time. After two years away the Expedition funds were exhausted, so that by early 1913 Edgar's family in Portsmouth were in straightened circumstances. They moved to Gower to stay with Edgar's parents-in-law, Mr and Mrs William Beynon, and during that time the news came through of his death.

Edgar had never intended his family to be in need while he was away: he had signed on in order to secure their future, since he was due to retire from the Navy within a few years. The Expedition's financial problems [11] were not his doing. Furthermore, to criticise Edgar for leaving Lois a widow and his children fatherless is being wise after the event. Did he neglect his family in pursuit of personal glory? Mr William Beynon, whose loyalty we might expect would be for his younger daughter Lois, said of his son-in-law, 'He was a fine boy. He was a good husband and a good son to his old mother'. [12] Lois herself said, 'He was such a good husband and how fond he was of the dear children. He had written, "A year will soon pass and then I shall be with you and the children once again".'

Furthermore, she said that her last communication from him comprised about fifty letters covering the period of a year. [13] A person who amid a busy schedule made the time to write an average of one letter a week was surely very aware of his responsibilities as a husband and a father. In the last dated of those letters he had written, 'I am always thinking of you on this great ice platform ten thousand feet above sea level'.

Thirdly, the circumstances of his death led some to feel that he 'let the side down'. Why was the 'strong man' the first to die? In his classic account of the expedition, *The Worst Journey in the World*, first published in 1922, Apsley Cherry-Garrard wrote:

> Evans's collapse... may have had something to do with the fact that he was the biggest, heaviest, and most muscular man in the party. I do not believe that this is a life for such men, who are expected to pull their weight and to support and drive a larger machine than their companions, and at the same time to eat no extra food. If, as seems likely, the ration these men were eating was not enough to support the work they were doing, then it is clear that the heaviest man will feel the deficiency sooner and more severely than others who are smaller than he. Evans must have had a most terrible time: I think it is clear from the diaries that he had suffered very greatly without complaint. At home he would have been nursed in bed: here he must march (he was pulling the day he died) until he was crawling on his frost bitten hands and knees in the snow — horrible: most horrible perhaps for those who found him so, and sat in the tent and watched him die. I am told that simple concussion does not kill as suddenly as this: probably some clot had moved in his brain.

Cherry-Garrard's final remark is borne out by the research of Dr A.F. Rogers (see page 81). Those who would concur with his opinion about the unsuitability of large men for a lengthy Antarctic sledging journey include Sir Ranulph Fiennes and Merthyr-born Dr Frank Davies, a member of Byrd's 1928–30 Antarctic Expedition. [14]

Although the question of scurvy among the Polar party is not proved, it is pertinent to quote Shackleton's comment when informed in New York of the tragedy, 'What is most to be feared is scurvy. That is the greatest danger of all Polar expeditions—far greater than any blizzard'. [15] Scurvy enfeebles a person long before bringing about his death. Its symptoms include swellings on the gums, blotches on the skin, a dull lethargy, mental depression and haemorrhages. If Edgar were suffering from incipient scurvy, those symptoms would not yet have been apparent, although the disease would have been taking its toll on the biggest man of the party. Scurvy had been eradicated in the Navy by 1795 when lemon juice was made compulsory issue, but re-appeared on polar expeditions in the nineteenth century, by which time lime juice (which has only half the antiscorbutic value of lemons) had been substituted for lemons. The true cause of scurvy —a deficiency of vitamin C—was only apparent when vitamins were discovered in 1912, too late to help Scott's party. [16]

In February 1913 a reporter found Edgar's widowed mother, Mrs Sarah Evans, distressed at the thought that her son's breakdown might have fatally slowed down the others: [17] this is a valid question. However, four days after Edgar's head injury in the crevasse fall, the five men had spent a morning collecting geological samples on the Beardmore Glacier, when the weather was good for travelling. If his condition had been impeding their progress they would surely have sacrificed scientific research in order to press on. I feel that any delay could have been only during the final day or two of his life, and Cherry-Garrard points out that Evans was in harness ready to pull the sledge on the day he died.

Edgar's daughter, Mrs Muriel Hawkins, said, 'I would have rather had a living father than a dead hero': [18] the tragedy is that in some people's eyes Edgar was not even that, for it was suggested that he went insane at the end. In New Zealand, Commander Evans, in charge of the Expedition after Scott's death, stated within a few days of the news of the tragedy that, 'the rumour that P.O. Evans became insane is wholly baseless. His illness was caused by privations and hardships, of which no man could be ashamed'. [19]

The rumour about insanity had arisen from the comment in Scott's journal, written the day before Edgar died, that 'Evans has nearly broken down in brain, we think'. There was no opportunity for Scott, writing in extremely difficult conditions in the tent, to amend or to expand on what he had written, but the subsequent research of Dr Rogers has thrown some light on that comment. The American playright, Ted Tally, depicts Edgar as being insane just before his death, in the play *Terra Nova*,[20] which was first performed at the Chichester Festival in 1980. A certain amount of artistic licence is also used in his portrayal of Captain Oates. Was Edgar—or any of them—'of a sound mind' a month after leaving the South Pole?

As recently as February 1993 Sir Ranulph Fiennes and Dr Michael Stroud, after the longest unsupported Antarctic journey, revealed something of the psychological pressure of such travelling. Fiennes admitted irrational antagonistic feelings towards his colleague for allegedly doing less work and having larger rations than he. Yet those two men knew each other well, had travelled together in both Arctic and Antarctic conditions, and had the advantages of current knowledge about vitamins and diet, using equipment as superior to that used by Scott's men as that of modern mountaineers is to equipment used by Mallory and Irvine. Fiennes and Stroud were described as 'more dead than alive' after their Antarctic sledging journey of three months. Edgar died after journeying for three and a half months, Oates for four and a half, and the others nearly five months: one wonders not so much why those five died, but that they lasted so long.

Some feel that Edgar was demoralised once they knew that Amundsen had reached the Pole first, as suggested by Sub-Lieutenant Gran's comment (p. 67). Obviously they could not envisage the immense wave of public feeling for them after the news of the tragedy, and it is only conjecture as to how they might have been received had they been able to return home alive.

Roland Huntford's weighty work, *Scott and Amundsen*, makes various uncomplimentary remarks about Edgar. In spite of a mass of references and footnotes, those particular observations are unsubstantiated, and correspondance with the author has failed to elucidate any corroboration. [21] Mr Huntford set out to correct what he perceives as the lack of appreciation by the British towards Amundsen's achievement, but his work shows extreme bias, for, in order to commend Amundsen, he constantly denigrates Scott and several people with him, such as Edgar. One of the co-biographers of Captain Oates, novelist Sue Limb, describes Mr Huntford's book as 'a masterpeice of iconoclasm'. One is not trying as a reaction to depict Edgar as some plaster cast saint (possibly Edward Wilson might be a subject approaching that category); Edgar was a real person, with human faults and failings, but Mr Huntford seems to portray him as the archetypal hard-drinking, loose-living sailor of popular imagination. We might assume that William Beynon would have some knowledge of any of his son-in-law's lapses, from his demeanour at the 'Ship Inn', yet he was always complimentary about Edgar.

Like the sinking of SS *Titanic* on her maiden voyage in April 1912, the story of Scott's Last Expedition is a peacetime tragedy that continues to fascinate and enthrall even after all these years. This book has sought to portray the Welsh seaman who played an integral part in that epic. He is ever linked with his four comrades from more privileged backgrounds, and now has been honoured in his home area during the lifetime of two of his three children. The people of Swansea, of Gower, and of South Wales can be proud of Chief Petty Officer Edgar Evans, RN.

NOTES

1. *SWEP*, 5 February 1962.

2. I am obliged to Dr Geoffrey Hattersley-Smith, and Mrs Ann Roberts of the British Antarctic Survey, for this information, which is taken from *Geographic Names of the Antarctic*, ed. G. Alberts (Washington, 1980).

3. *Portsmouth Evening News*, 18 December 1964.

4. *Herald of Wales*, 29 January 1966.

5. *SWEP*, 6 April 1966.

6. ibid., 24 September 1971.

7. ibid., 5 November 1984.

8. Michael Tarver of the Captain Scott Society organised this memorable occasion.

9. *SWEP*, 3 July 1994. The pupils presented an excellent 'This is your life' about Edgar, written by Headmaster Philip Andrew.

10. *SWEP*, 2 November 1994.

11. On 11 October 1911, Captain Scott invited the officers and scientists to forego their pay for the next twelve months. All but a few, who could not afford to, did so.

12. *SWDP*, 11 February 1913.

13. ibid., 14 February 1913.

14. Letter from Geoffrey Hattersley-Smith, 25 April 1994.

15. *SWDP*, 12 February 1913.

16. *Oxford Companion to Ships and the Sea* (London, 1976).

17. *SWDP*, 19 February 1913.

18. Conversation with the author on 7 January 1994.

19. *WM*, 17 February 1913.

20. I am obliged to Mark Smith, of the Captain Scott society.

21. Letter to the author, 20 July 1993.

CHAPTER 10

The Best Choice?

Who should have gone to the Pole? With the benefit of hindsight, a case can be made out for various permutations for the party to mount the final assault on the Pole, each having theoretically the promise of returning successfully. But as Wilfred Wooller, former captain and secretary of Glamorgan County Cricket Club, and a test selector,[1] has said, 'The armchair selector has this advantage: his or her team never has to actually take the field'.

The most radical suggestion would be for Meares to have taken the dog teams onto the Plateau. But the British Expedition never imagined that this was a viable alternative, even allowing for the superior prowess of the Norwegians in handling dog teams. Scott was amazed to see signs that the Norwegians had managed to get their dogs right to the Pole. Even writing ten years later, Cherry-Garrard, in *The Worst Journey in the World*, doubted the feasibility of taking dogs up and down the Beardmore Glacier.

Of the last eight men, Lieutenant Evans and Stoker Lashly had done several hundred more miles of man-hauling (since the motor sledges had broken down), and it was surely beyond even their indominatable spirits to haul a sledge on to the Pole and all the long journey back to base.

That left six men, and on 3 January 1912, Scott did not have the benefit of knowing what PO Crean would achieve on the return to Hut Point, nor the part he would play in the epic journey in the *James Caird* with Shackleton in 1915, and the subsequent march across South Georgia.

Although Atkinson and Oates might have preferred another of the seamen, Scott had no reason to doubt Edgar's suitability, as was borne out by Ponting's observation. One might feel that Edgar could have declared his hand injury, but he probably felt that he could cope notwithstanding that.

Therefore the final choice could hardly differ from Scott's, apart from one vital element—that of taking five men instead of four. He may have decided to take on *his* team of four (Scott, Wilson, Oates and Edgar), for he had ordered the other four men to deposit their skis earlier, for collection on the return journey; did Scott alter his plans in response to Bowers's reaction? To make such a crucial re-arrangement because of a junior officer's reaction seems incredible. Certainly Bowers had shown his suitability, both on the winter journey with Wilson and Cherry-Garrard, and by the way he had worked hitherto on the Southern Journey, and he was to thoroughly vindicate the decision to include him in the polar party.

If anything one feels that Oates might have returned with the Last Support Party, but Scott wanted a representative of the Army at the Pole, and to reward him for his excellent work in getting the Manchurian ponies across the Barrier. Besides, even if by 3 January Oates felt that he had had enough, the honour of his regiment was enough motivation for him to carry on, and he had proved in the Cape that he was not one to give up.

Geologist Raymond Priestley (who had previously been with Shackleton in the *Nimrod*) suggested that Edgar was at a disadvantage in the polar party. He said, 'The psychological effect of being, in those days, a rating among four officers, placed a heavy burden on poor Evans. He was in a thought compartment by himself, and was naturally the first to crack'. But this is refuted by Frank Debenham, who said that Priestley was hardly ever with Edgar, and added,

> Taff was quite at ease with officers, and would never have felt the least barrier with his sledging companions, though he was always very correct in addressing them. And of course it's quite nonsense for anyone to suggest that he, or any other member of the mess deck, was ever screened off from the officers when sledging, we were always in complete harmony. ...I should say that Taff got on well with all the officers, except Lieut. Evans, who never quite forgave him for one of his 'drinking too much' occasions in New Zealand. [2]

It is mere conjecture whether any four or five out of those exceptional eight men left after the First Support Party turned back would have made any difference. Many factors contributed to the tragedy, each one relatively unimportant in itself, yet the sum total meant that all five men who were photographed at the South Pole on 18 January 1912 perished on that return journey.

NOTES

1. Wilfred Wooller also captained Wales at rugby before the Second World War.
2. SM: letter of 25 May 1962.

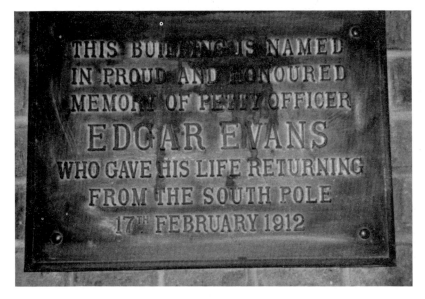

Figure 23.   Plaque in the foyer of the Edgar Evans Building, Whale Island, Portsmouth.
(Jane Gregor)

CHRONOLOGY

1862, 24 July:	wedding of Charles Evans and Sarah Beynon
1876, 7 March:	Edgar Evans born in Middleton
1883–1889:	attends St Helen's School, Swansea
1891:	joins the Royal Navy; training in HMS *Ganges*, Falmouth
1899–1901:	serves in HMS *Majestic*, meeting Lieutenant Scott
1901–1904:	the *Discovery* expedition
1903:	the 'Western Journey', with Scott and Lashly
1904, 10 September:	returns to Britain
1904, 13 December:	marriage to Lois Beynon at Rhosili church
1905:	Gunnery Instructor at HMS *Excellent*, Portsmouth
1906, 1907:	his gun crews win the Royal Naval Tattoo for Field Gunnery at the White City, London
1910, 15 June:	sails from Cardiff in the *Terra Nova*
1911, 1 November:	commencement of the 'Southern Journey'
1912, 17 January:	reaches the South Pole
1912, 4 February:	head injury in crevasse fall
1912, 17 February:	death near Monument Rock, aged thirty-five
1912, 12 November:	bodies of Scott, Wilson and Bowers found
1913, 10 February:	first news of tragedy reaches Swansea
1914, 27 January:	memorial tablet in Rhosili church
1921, 1 March:	picture presented to St Helen's School, Swansea

1948, 30 December:	members of family attend premiere of film, *Scott of the Antarctic*
1952, 23 April:	death of Mrs Lois Evans
1957:	New Zealand expedition names the Evans Piedmont Glacier
1961–62:	the Evans Glacier named in Antarctica
1962:	Mr Stanley Richards begins campaign for a local memorial
1963–64:	Evans Névé named in Antarctica
1964, 18 December:	Edgar Evans Building opened in Portsmouth
1966:	two paintings presented to Swansea Museum
1974:	article about Evans's death in *The Practitioner*
1978:	memorial oak chair presented to St Mary's church, Swansea
1993:	Swansea Museum exhibition and booklet
1994, 17 February:	Civic Ceremony and presentation of bust at the Brangwyn Hall, Swansea
1994, 30 June:	opening of display at St Helen's School, Swansea

SLEDGE PARTIES
(relevant to this narrative)

The First Geological Party (4): January–March 1911
T. Griffith Taylor
Charles S. Wright
Frank Debenham
P.O. Edgar Evans*

The Northern Party (6):
Lieutenant Victor L.A. Campbell
Surgeon G. Murray Levick
Raymond E. Priestley
P.O. George Abbott
P.O. Frank V. Browning
Henry Dickason

The Winter Journey (3): July–August 1911
Dr Edward A. Wilson*
Lieutenant Henry R. Bowers
Apsley Cherry-Garrard

The Dog Teams (2):
Cecil H. Meares
Dimitri Gerop

The Motor Party (4):
Lieutenant Edward R.G.R. Evans
Chief Stoker William Lashly*

Bernard C.Day
F.J. Hooper

The First Support Party (4): November 1911–January 1912
Surgeon Edward L. Atkinson
Charles S. Wright
Apsley Cherry-Garrard
P.O. Patrick Keohane

The Second Support Party (3): November 1911–February 1912
Lieutenant Edward R.G.R. Evans
Chief Stoker William Lashly*
P.O. Thomas Crean*

The Polar Party (5): November 1911–March 1912
Captain Robert F. Scott*
Dr Edward A. Wilson*
Captain Lawrence E.G. Oates
Lieutenant Henry R. Bowers
P.O. Edgar Evans*

The Relief Expedition (11): October–December 1912
Surgeon Edward L. Atkinson
Sub-Lieutenant Tryggve Gran
Charles S. Wright
Apsley Cherry-Garrard
Chief Stoker William Lashly*
P.O. Thomas Crean*
P.O. Patrick Keohane
P.O. Thomas S.Williamson*
Edward W. Nelson
F.J. Hooper
Dimitri Gerop

(Frank Debenham and W.W. Archer remained at the hut)

* Veterans of the 1901–4 *Discovery* Expedition.

'The Martyred Hero of Antarctica'

Edgar Evans still unhonoured in his native Wales

(By H. Stanley Richards)[1]

Unaccountably the name of this valiant does not appear in the *Welsh Dictionary of National Biography*;[2] stranger still, he has not yet been commemorated by Swansea and district.

Edgar Evans was born in Rhosili, Gower, in 1876, but left when a very young boy to live in Swansea where he attended school and from there in 1891 joined the Royal Navy. In 1901 he volunteered to accompany Captain Robert Falcon Scott on his first venture to Antarctica. In 1906, and again in 1907, when a gunnery instructor, he and his gun-crew won the Naval Tattoo for field-gunnery at the White City, London. But it was on Scott's second expedition which set out from Cardiff in the *Terra Nova* in 1910 that Edgar rose to heights of glory.

Strength, Resourcefulness and Capability

There is an amusing local anecdote told of him and his immense strength. During one of his leave periods from the Royal Navy while he was staying at the Ship Inn in Middleton, Rhosili, with his wife Lois, who was his first cousin and the daughter of the innkeeper, Mr Beynon, a picnic party arrived from Swansea in a horse-break [an open waggon with bench seats]. After spending a few hours at the inn, several of the visitors became very much out of control and the landlord called upon his nephew for assistance. In a very short time Edgar Evans had cleared the bar, escorting the trouble-makers into the open air two at a time, and dealing with them in such a manner that they swore they would never visit the inn again!

Edgar was highly admired from many angles by his colleagues, and was particularly renowned as the strong man of Scott's party. Said Griffith Taylor, the geologist, 'The other room was almost filled with a huge petty officer who was sorting gear for the sledges. I looked at his sturdy proportions with considerable respect, which would have been increased had I known how invaluable "Taff" Evans was to be on my first expedition to the Antarctic.'

Scott's tributes continued to the end:

> Evans shows himself wonderfully capable and I haven't a doubt as to the working of the sledges he has fitted up.

> The party gives Evans a very high character.

> … but the greatest source of pleasure to me is to realise that I have such men as Bowers and P.O. Evans for the southern journey. I do not think that hardier men or better sledge travellers ever took the trail.

> Edgar Evans looks after our sledges and sledge equipment with a care and management and a fertility of resource which is truly astonishing.

> Evans, a giant worker with a really remarkable head-piece. It is now I realise how much has been due to him.'

Anecdotal, humourous and cheerful

Scott and other officers maintain that Edgar had an inexhaustible supply of anecdotes, was very humourous, and unendingly cheerful:

> Seaman Evans had read many popular works, and was far superior in this respect to any of the other seamen with whom I had much to do. He had read some of Kipling's poems and 'had no use for them' nor did Dickens appeal to him. As was perhaps natural, he preferred works with more 'plot' in them; especially did he delight in the works of the French writer whose name he anglicised as Dum-ass!

> We were tugging ourselves to bits through very deep snow and we had to halt for breath and, after heaving, the rest of us used every kind of damn we could think of. Taff looked at the feet of soft snow and said, 'The Curse of the Seven Blind Witches of Egypt be upon you!' turning our wrath to laughter.

Scientific investigations, afterwards the Pole

Scott, whom Edgar idolised, was imbued primarily with scientific investigation. Reaching the South Pole was of secondary importance.[3] As a consequence of this decision his findings are a monument to him and have proved a great boon to others who followed in his tracks, so that rightly he is the uncrowned King of Antarctica. Although he knew that Amundsen would probably reach the Pole before him, this did not deter him from finishing off his scientific quest.

Delays occurred, but worse than all was the unprecedented foul weather even blizzards and gales setting in early and ferociously. For part of the journey south, Scott was accompanied by his second-in-command, Lieutenant Edward Evans and two others but Scott told them to return; so it was Scott, Edgar Evans, Bowers, Oates and Dr Wilson who journeyed on. Teddy Evans has been confused with Edgar Evans, but Cardiff's Fighting Sailor (afterwards the famous Evans of the Broke, etc.) did not visit the Pole and so survived.

The story of Scott's Last Expedition is a saga of fortitude under great trials and appalling conditions. Very soon after setting out, Edgar Evans sustained a cut hand in the course of his technical work, and this was to prove fatal to him.

They reached the Pole only to find that Amundsen had forestalled them. It was a bitter pill to swallow, particularly as they had endured such privations on the way. 'Great God!' said Scott, 'This is an awful place and terrible enough for us to have laboured without the reward of priority'.

Death the merciful
Even before reaching the Pole Edgar's hand was giving him much trouble, though he never complained. By then it was suppurating and he knew that it would never heal under such dreadful conditions. At first he was angry with himself for having incurred the wound, later on he lost his cheerfulness and became dejected because he thought he had let down his chief by having that accident and he feared that he would delay the party. On the return journey he twice fell into crevasses and injured his brain. But even on the last day that he lived he maintained that he was quite all right. The effect of a cut hand on any of the others would have been at least the same, probably even worse than on the strong man. It was his injured hand and brain damage which finally cut him down.

Wrote Scott, 'I was the first to reach the poor man and shocked at his appearance: he was on his knees with clothing disarranged, hands uncovered and frostbitten and a wild look in his eyes. Asked what was the matter, he replied with a slow speech that he didn't know, but thought he must have fainted.' He passed away in a coma a few hours later, on 18 February,[4] 1912, in the early morning.

It is in this connection that some critics have blamed Edgar Evans, for they consider that he had let down the party. It is true that Scott and his companions felt the loss of their strong man very keenly. But Edgar could not help that death claimed him, mercifully too, so this contention is absurd. Had both Evans and Oates lived, and even if the party had reached One-Ton Camp safely, where there was a supply of food, their doom was sealed because of the continued severity of the weather.

It was Amundsen who at first won the glory, but with the passage of time it is Scott's great work and the fortitude of him and his men which have stood the test of time, and for ever will be remembered as deeds of sublime service and valour.

Now is the hour

Edgar did not forget Wales in Antarctica for he named a certain physical feature the Wales Glacier. But Wales, and in particular Swansea District, has not yet raised a memorial to him. Dr Wilson, not so renowned and colourful as Edgar, very deservedly has a monument to himself in Gloucester.[5] The only one erected to our hero in Wales is a small plaque in Rhosili Church, paid for by his widow out of her meagre pension.[6]

On 18 December, 1964 however, the Royal Navy named a fine new edifice in HMS *Excellent*, Whale Island, Portsmouth, the 'Edgar Evans Building' and a plaque was unveiled to his memory. At the opening ceremony, Admiral Sir Royston Wright, Chief of Naval Personnel and Second Sea Lord, stated that naval establishments are usually called after famous admirals, but that this building was the first named after a petty officer, and this was absolutely correct and most appropriate. He added that Edgar Evans was again chosen by Scott for the second expedition because he was a big, splendid, strong man, with strength of character, devotion, loyalty and bravery.

It is never too late to honour a great worthy, and it is to be hoped that Swansea will rise to the occasion by erecting a memorial to Edgar Evans, say in Castle Gardens. He will for ever be in Swansea's memory because he rose to such great heights in human endeavour and forged an indissoluble link between Swansea and Antarctica, but as long as he is neglected he will remain on Swansea's conscious also so that to many people he will continue to be the martyred hero of Antarctica.

'To seek, to strive, to find, and not to yield' was so typical of the venturesome career of this redoubtable Welshman.

NOTES

1. Mr Richards was Curator of Swansea Museum (see page 78). This article appeared in *SWEP*, 1 and 2 February 1966.

2. The correct title of this work is *The Dictionary of Welsh Biography down to 1940* (London, 1959), itself derived from the earlier Welsh language version, *Y Bywgraffiadur Cymreig hyd 1940* (Llundain, 1953). Richards has mixed up the title with that of the great reference work on British biography, the *Dictionary of National Biography*, from which Evans was also omitted.

3. To say that for Scott 'reaching the South Pole was of secondary importance' is debatable. It is to Scott's credit that he did not curtail the scientific programme after hearing that Amundsen was starting from the Bay of Whales. But priority at the Pole was a vital factor in terms of national pride and making up the expedition's substantial financial outlay.

4. 18 February is given as the date of Evans's death, from Scott's statement of 17 February that 'He died quietly at 12.30 am'. However Wilson wrote 'He died without recovering consciousness that night about 10.00 p.m.', so that 17 February is generally the accepted date.

5. The memorial to Dr Wilson is in Cheltenham, not Gloucester.

6. The mention of Mrs Evans's 'meagre pension' contrasts with her statement that she was well satisfied with the provisions from the Mansion House fund for her and the children (see page 73). Admittedly compared to that of Lady Scott her pension was small.

APPENDIX 4:

Locations of Edgar Evans Memorabilia

HMS *Excellent*, Whale Island, Portsmouth:
Skis, display.

Royal Mail, Phoenix Way, Swansea:
H.A. Chapman's photograph of 1904.

St Helen's School, Vincent Street, Swansea:
Plaster head (Philip Chatfield), framed photograph, display of children's work.

St Mary's Church, Rhosili:
Memorial tablet.

St Mary's Church, Swansea:
Oak chair (Gwyn Morris).

Swansea Museum, Victoria Road, Swansea:
Bust (Philip Chatfield), two oil paintings (John J. Jones), plaster figurine (George Evans), boot, display.

Select Bibiliography

UNPUBLISHED

Documents were consulted at Swansea Museum, Swansea Central Refence Library, the Scott Polar Research Institute, Cambridge, and the Oates Museum, Selborne. There was also assistance at Discovery Point, Dundee, and HMS *Excellent*, Portsmouth.

BOOKS

BAINBRIDGE, B., *The Birthday Boys* (London, 1991).

BERNACCHI, L.C., *The Saga of the Discovery* (London, 1938).

CHERRY-GARRARD, A., *The Worst Journey in the World* (London, 1922).

DEBENHAM, F., *Antarctica* (London, 1959).

ELLIS, A.R. (ed.), *Under Scott's Command* [Lashly's Diaries] (London, 1969).

EVANS, E.G.R., *South With Scott* (London, 1921).

HATTERSLEY-SMITH, G. (ed.), *The Norwegian with Scott* [Gran's Diaries] (HMSO, London, 1984).

HUNTFORD, R., *Scott and Amundsen* (London, 1979).

HUXLEY, E., *Scott of the Antarctic* (London, 1977).

LIMB, S. and CORDINGLEY, P., *Captain Oates, Soldier and Explorer* (London, 1982).

POUND, R., *Scott of the Antarctic* (London, 1966).

SAVOURS, A. (ed.), *Scott's Last Voyage* (London, 1974).

SCOTT, R.F., *The Voyage of the Discovery* (London, 1905).

SCOTT, R.F., (ed. L. Huxley) *Scott's Last Expedition* (London, 1913).

SEAVER, G., *Edward Wilson of the Antarctic* (London, 1933).

SHACKLETON, E., *South* (London, 1919).

STROUD, M., *Shadows on the Wasteland* (London, 1993).

TARVER, C.M., *The Captain Scott Society* (Cardiff, 1990).

THOMSON, D., *Scott's Men* (London, 1977).

ARTICLES

BEVAN, D., 'In Search of a Local Hero', *Rhosili Community Council Newsletter* (January–February 1987).

GREGOR, G.C., 'Edgar Evans: From Worm's Head to South Pole', *Gower*, xliv (1993), 21–33, and xlv (1994), 90–4.

JOHNSON, A.M., 'Scott of the Antarctic and Cardiff', *Morgannwg*, xxvi (1982), 15–52, and xxvii (1983), 25–58.

LEE, S., 'The Population of Rhosili', *Gower*, iv (1951), 27.

LUCAS, R., 'A Few Little Plans.... Some Sidelights on Rhosili in the 1880s and 90s, *Gower*, xliv (1993), 57–70.

ROGERS, A.F., 'The Death of C.P.O. Evans', *The Practitioner* (1974), 570–80.

NEWSPAPERS, ETC.

The *Cambrian.*

Cambria Daily Leader.

Gower Church Magazine.

South Wales Daily News.

South Wales Daily Post.

South Wales Evening Post.

Western Mail.

Studies in Swansea's History

OTHER TITLES IN THE SERIES

1. R.T. Price, *Little Ireland. Aspects of the Irish and Greenhill, Swansea* (1992). xvi + 159 pp. Illustrated. £8.50.

2. N.A. Robins, *Homes for Heroes. Early Twentieth-Century Council Housing in the County Borough of Swansea* (1992). xxii + 84 pp. Illustrated. £6.00.

3. J.R. Alban, *The 'Three Nights' Blitz'. Select Contemporary Reports relating to Swansea's Air Raids of February 1941* (1994). xvi + 179 pp. Illustrated. £9.50.